CORPORATE PHILOSOPHIES AND MISSION STATEMENTS

Recent Titles from Quorum Books

Strategic Organization Planning: Downsizing for Survival
David C. Dougherty

Joint Venture Partner Selection: Strategies for Developed Countries
J. Michael Geringer

Sustainable Corporate Growth: A Model and Management Planning
Tool
John J. Clark, Thomas C. Chiang, and Gerard T. Olson

Competitive Freedom Versus National Security Regulation
Manley Rutherford Irwin

Labor Law and Business Change: Theoretical and Transactional
Perspectives
Samuel Estreicher and Daniel G. Collins, eds.

The Constitutional Right to a Speedy and Fair Criminal Trial
Warren Freedman

Entrepreneurial Systems for the 1990s: Their Creation, Structure, and
Management
John E. Tropman and Gersh Morningstar

From Organizational Decline to Organizational Renewal: The Phoenix
Syndrome
Mary E. Guy

Modern Analytical Auditing: Practical Guidance for Auditors and
Accountants
Thomas E. McKee

Multiple Use Job Descriptions: A Guide to Analysis, Preparation, and
Applications for Human Resources Managers
Philip C. Grant

Cost-Effective Marketing Research: A Guide for Marketing Managers
Eric J. Soares

Corporate Philosophies and Mission Statements

A Survey and Guide for Corporate Communicators and Management

THOMAS A. FALSEY

Q

QUORUM BOOKS

New York • Westport, Connecticut • London

Library of Congress Cataloging-in-Publication Data

Falsey, Thomas A.
 Corporate philosophies and mission statements : a survey and guide
for corporate communicators and management / Thomas A. Falsey.
   p. cm.
 Includes index.
 ISBN 0–89930–313–7 (lib. bdg. : alk. paper)
 1. Corporate culture. I. Title. II. Title: Mission statements.
HD58.7.F35   1989
658.4′012—dc19   88–18257

British Library Cataloguing in Publication Data is available.

Library of Congress Catalog Card Number: 88–18257
ISBN: 0–89930–313–7

First published in 1989 by Quorum Books

Greenwood Press, Inc.
88 Post Road West, Westport, Connecticut   06881

Printed in the United States of America

∞™

The paper used in this book complies with the
Permanent Paper Standard issued by the National
Information Standards Organization (Z39.48–1984).

10 9 8 7 6 5 4 3 2 1

3-4-90

Contents

Introduction

Although I had seen a number of mission statements in my life, I was never very impressed with them. They seemed to be too idealistic to be believable. I wasn't quite sure how much of what they said could actually be true.

On September 28, 1982, something happened that changed my thinking about mission statements. It was on this day I learned that seven people in Chicago had died after taking Extra Strength TYLENOL® capsules laced with cyanide poisoning. Like the rest of the world, I was shocked. I was shocked not only because this did happen, but also because this *could* happen.

The poisonings changed many things. They changed Johnson & Johnson. They changed the pharmaceutical industry. They also changed the packaging industry. In many ways, the poisonings changed the thinking of almost all of us. For the first time, many of us felt extremely vulnerable. What happened in Chicago could happen anywhere. What happened to TYLENOL® could happen to any product. What was once taken for granted, was now a concern.

As the facts became known about the poisonings, many questions arose. Could Johnson & Johnson survive this incident? Could any company? They were facing a $100,000,000 loss. Could they ever rebuild from this? Could TYLENOL® survive? It was their largest selling and most profitable product. Would the company regain the trust of their customers? Only time would answer these questions. It was too early for answers. There were just more questions.

For me, there was one additional question. One that hit closer to home. I was working for Johnson & Johnson at the time. I was worried about my job. Would it survive?

In the months that followed Johnson & Johnson did a remarkable job of recovering from this tragedy. In a few months they rebuilt the brand and relaunched the product. The public showed their support for the company by continuing to buy the product after it was reintroduced. The press and the public had only praise for the company and how it had conducted its business during these uncertain times.

After the dust had settled, there was ample opportunity for Johnson & Johnson to take credit for its actions. Yet the management of the company did not praise themselves for their actions; instead they gave much of the credit to a company philosophy. The management of Johnson & Johnson credited their corporate philosophy, "Our Credo," for guiding them through this crisis.

I found this rather strange. I had seen the Credo on many occasions, but it never meant much to me. It was posted on the wall in our lobby. It was written up in the annual report. I even had a copy of it over my desk. But in truth, it never meant that much to me before the poisonings.

When the company gave so much credit to the Credo, I became curious. Was the Credo really that important in helping the company react the way they did? Or was this simply a way of getting good publicity from a very unfortunate incident?

I read the Credo again. This time, for perhaps the first time, I really *read* it. This time it meant something to me. This time I believed in what it said. I believed in what it did for the company. Now it meant a great deal to me. I had seen the Credo in action. It had been tested, and it worked.

Before the poisonings, I had a great deal of admiration for the management of Johnson & Johnson. After the poisonings, I had a great deal more. I also had a lot of pride—pride in the management and in the company's management philosophy.

I began to study mission statements. I looked for them. I asked a lot of questions about them. I learned that Johnson & Johnson is not unique. Many companies have mission statements. They are all different, but they have similarities too.

Some companies consider them confidential. Others proudly display them whenever and wherever they have the opportunity.

Some people believe in mission statements. Others are skeptical.

To me, a mission statement is only important if the words are backed up with action. I don't care what a company says about itself. I care about what it does. I don't care if there is a written document which is called the "mission statement." I care if there is a management philosophy that is followed. The true test comes when things get tough. That is when the company's true character is most evident.

Like most people, I sincerely hope that no company is ever again tested like Johnson & Johnson was tested in the moments that followed the poisonings. I hope we will never know how any other company would react under these circumstances. Yet I take comfort in knowing how one company did react.

The words of a mission statement make for good public relations. To some, they may mean little more than that. A mission statement tells what a company wants to be. It tells how the company wants to be judged. While some of these companies live up to their commitments, others may not. I believe it is important to look at the intent of these documents.

In putting this book together, I had to rely on many companies. All of the missions printed here are reprinted with the permission of the companies that own them. Most gave their permission without questioning my intent.

It would be easy to lose sight of the intention of this book. It would be possible to find examples of how a given company did *not* live up to their mission statement. It would be easy to second guess people after the fact. Such is not my intent, however.

In granting me permission to reprint these documents, many companies placed their trust in me. Perhaps I praise some of these companies too much in this book. However, the praise is for the intent of what is being said. And I believe in most cases the honest intent of these documents is good.

CORPORATE PHILOSOPHIES AND MISSION STATEMENTS

1

What Is a Mission Statement?

In looking at successful companies, one can find many threads that tie their achievements together. There are elements that they all have in common. There are elements separating them, thereby making each company unique.

Success breeds success. When new companies form they try to improve on other companies to find their own little niche. Certain things will be done to imitate the best companies, other things will be done to set them apart.

While there may be no magic formula that makes companies successful, there are certain characteristics that are often imitated. Perhaps the thought is that if so many successful companies are doing one thing there may be something to it.

One such thing that is often imitated is the setting of a written, codified set of principles by which the company is to be run. Although these documents go by various names, they can all be called mission statements.

"Mission statement" can mean many different things to people. The development of a mission statement can be both challenging and time consuming. Yet, many companies feel that the mission statement is a useful document that is at the heart of their corporate philosophy.

In a mission statement a company puts itself up for public scrutiny. The mission statement will be judged and evaluated by those who read it. It will be evaluated for what it says and how the company lives up to what it says. Knowing this, why would any company write a mission statement? Why would a company provide a yardstick by which others might measure them?

Many companies feel it is important to have a codified set of principles to guide their actions. They feel this is important despite the fact that it may open them to unsolicited criticism— both positive and negative.

Harsco Corporation

MISSION

The mission of Harsco Corporation is to be a leading international manufacturer, marketer and distributor of diverse goods and services principally for industrial, commercial, construction and defense applications. The Corporation is committed to providing innovative engineering solutions to specialized problems where technology and close attention to customer service can differentiate it from commodity production or job-shop operations. In accomplishing its mission, the Corporation will build upon the base of experience acquired during its long association with metalworking. Growth will be achieved both through acquisition and internal development within a framework that balances the risk of diversification against the continued prudent management of current businesses.

Exhibit 1. Harsco Corporation's "Mission"

Kimberly Clark Company

Four principles which the Kimberly Clark Company was founded upon:

—Manufacture the best possible product.
—Serve the customers well and deal fairly to gain their confidence and good will.
—Deal fairly with employees.
—Expand capacity as demand for product justifies; finance expansion out of earnings.

Exhibit 2. Kimberly Clark Company's Four Principles

The term "mission statement" can be defined several ways. In fact, there are probably as many definitions as there are companies that have them. Perhaps the simplest definition is that a mission statement tells two things about a company: who it is and what it does.

A mission statement, almost by definition, says very positive things. This point is understandable when you consider its origin. A company writes its own mission statement. It is written by people who work for, and are

---

Message from the Publisher

The goals of McCormick and Company, Inc., the owner and publisher of the Town Talk, can be stated very simply:

—To provide the people of Central Louisiana with a good daily newspaper.

—To make available to our readers a balanced, comprehensive news report with a strong emphasis on local and area coverage.

—To critically observe and comment on events, institutions, and personalities in a fair, reasonable manner.

—To provide an open forum for reader comment and opinion.

—To supply readers with information that can be helpful and useful in our increasingly complex society.

—To serve advertisers as the most efficient, effective medium of advertising.

—To employ and advance individuals of demonstrated ability and performance and to reward them according to their contribution to the success of our endeavors.

—To foster and promote the healthy development of Alexandria-Pineville and the area with corresponding benefits for all its citizens.

—To make a sufficient profit to pay the company owners a reasonable return on their investment and to retain earnings adequate for economic independence and to provide facilities and equipment for future growth and development.

Joe D. Smith, Jr.
President and Publisher
(March, 1983)

Exhibit 3. McCormick and Company's "Message from the Publisher"

Corporate Mission

At Baxter Travenol, we seek to offer the best products, systems and services to health-care providers around the world, enabling them to deliver quality care more efficiently. To realize this goal, we will:

- provide quality and value in the goods and services we offer our customers;
- establish and maintain leadership positions in the health-care markets we serve, and
- promote an environment for employees that fosters teamwork, personal growth and respect for the individual.

Achieving these objectives will serve health-care needs worldwide and increase the value of our stockholders' investments.

Exhibit 4. Baxter Travenol Laboratories' "Corporate Mission"

paid by, the company. Often the mission statement will be etched in bronze, and displayed on the walls of corporate headquarters. It is quite unlikely therefore that it would be written to say anything negative about the company.

Because the mission statement is written internally, it can be somewhat biased. Before discounting the value of a mission statement, however, it might be wise to look at the companies who have written them. Many of this country's most successful companies have mission statements and believe firmly in them. It seems logical that they must have good reason for doing so.

For the purpose of this book, the term "mission statement" will be used as a generic term. The documents examined will have many different names including corporate philosophies, credos, guidelines, our purpose, and so on. All of these documents will be referred to as mission statements.

Although there are many different names, all of these documents have something in common. They tell something about the character and the priorities of the company. The purpose of this book is to evaluate these mission statements objectively, to see what they have in common, and to see what sets them apart.

Strictly stated, there are several documents included in this book that are not mission statements. For example, "Foundations for an Uncommon Company" is not the mission statement of Marion Laboratories, nor is "The Priceless Ingredient" the mission statement of Squibb Corporation. Both of these companies have other documents that could be more accurately called "the mission statement." However, all of these documents are included here because they fit the definition set forth above.

The value of a mission statement could be debated for hours. Valid points could be made both for and against their value. However, the true test of a company can be found by evaluating its success: is the company truly successful in achieving what it sets out to do?

Rather than attempting to convince you of the value of mission statements, we will look at company track records. To do this, we will look at several of this country's most successful companies, all of which have mission statements, and let their success speak for itself. These companies include the following:

> At Johnson & Johnson the mission statement is entitled, "Our Credo." It was this document that helped the company turn tragedy into triumph when dealing with the recall and relaunch of its largest selling product (TYLENOL®) after it had been tainted with cyanide.

> For Apple Computer, the company's philosophy is set forth in "Apple Values." Following these values the company went from inception to inclusion in the *Fortune* 500 faster than any other company in history.

> The associates of Marion Laboratories follow the ideals of "Foundations for an Uncommon Company." Over the past five years its sales have increased 390 percent, while the value of its stock has increased 2600 percent.

For these companies, and for many others like them, the ideals set forth in these documents are more than just words. They are documents intended to guide the thoughts and actions of employees. They outline the goals by which a company wants to be measured, and they tell where the company's priorities lie.

A mission statement is not magical. There is certainly no guarantee that drafting one will help a company improve its performance.

Similarly, there is no reason to expect that a company without a mission statement is not a successful company. There are many companies without mission statements that are rightfully considered highly successful.

There is one point, however, that remains clear. When so many of the best-performing and most respected companies have mission statements, there may be something to be learned by examining them.

There is an old philosophy that states, if you want to be rich, watch what poor people do and don't follow their example. It seems equally logical that if you want to be successful, look at others who are successful, and imitate them.

The idea of drafting a mission is not new. Examples have been around for generations. It would be difficult to trace accurately the history of mission statements. This is due in part to the fact that the term "mission statement" is abstract. As we shall see in a later chapter, there are examples of mission statements dating back to biblical times.

Examining all of the mission statements ever written would clearly be a difficult, if not impossible, task. In this book, we will be concentrating on mission statements of American corporations. Although we will look at a few specific examples of mission statements in history, we will not dwell on those documents. We will concentrate on the mission statements of current companies headquartered in this country.

About one hundred years ago, The Northwestern Mutual Life Insurance Company drafted its first mission statement (Exhibit 8). It was first written in 1888. Although this document is quite old, the words, the philosophy, and the thoughts of that document are still as appropriate today as when they were first written.

Does Northwestern Mutual live by its philosophy? Did it ever? Again, let's look at the record. The company has been in existence for over 100 years. That fact alone separates Northwestern from most other companies in the *Fortune* 500.

Johnson Controls

CORPORATE CREED

We believe in the free enterprise system, and we shall consistently treat our customers, employees, stockholders, suppliers, and community with honesty, dignity, fairness, and respect. We will conduct our business with the highest ethical standards.

Exhibit 5. Johnson Controls' "Corporate Creed"

Lever Brothers

The mission of our company

As William Hesketh Lever saw it

Is to make cleanliness commonplace

To lessen work for women

To foster health and

Contribute to personal attractiveness

That life may be more enjoyable

And rewarding for the people

Who use our products

Lever Brothers Company

Exhibit 6. Lever Brothers Mission

It may be impossible to determine if Northwestern Mutual would be any different without a mission statement. It would also be impossible to say whether they would be better or worse without this document. However, the company has done more than survive, it has flourished. The company has existed for more than one hundred years in a highly competitive industry.

There are few things in life that are permanent. Times change, managements change, and priorities change. Mission statements too, change. To be of maximum value, they must evolve to keep current with the changes that occur around them.

Maybe it would be a more accurate statement to say that mission statements evolve. The changes can appear so minor that they go unnoticed, or they can be major, perhaps signaling a significant change in the direction of the company. But they do change to reflect the current thinking and priorities of the corporation. To get a feel for why missions change, we will look at some comments made by John McKinley, former chairman of Texaco, in the preface of "Texaco's Guiding Principles and Objectives":

Since the Company was first organized in 1902, it has operated upon the basis of firmly established principles and sound corporate objectives. Many of these were laid down by the founders of the Company. Others have been formulated by management in succeeding periods. Some were written, some spoken, and others only generally understood or implied. . . .

As the Company continues to expand it is important to restate these principles and objectives from time to time so that they will be readily available for the guidance of all employees.

The evolution of a mission statement involves more than an evolution of words. It involves the evolution of ideas, language, and priorities. It also involves changes in management, changes in personnel, and more.

A mission statement need not be a long, involved document. It can be any length as long as it properly represents the ideas intended by its authors. For some the document may consist of several pages, while for others, a short simple idea is adequate.

Stanley Works

Our nearly century and a half of success has been built on four pillars:

- Making available to our customers needed products and services of real *value*.
- Conducting all of our business and community relations with *integrity*.
- Treating our employees, suppliers, customers and all with whom we associate with *respect*.
- In all matters, whether it be the products we make, the services we provide, the people we hire or the way we conduct ourselves—to make certain that quality is the glue that holds together everything that happens here at Stanley.

Excerpt from letter to employees December 19, 1983

The Stanley Works

Exhibit 7. The Stanley Works, Letter to Employees

The Northwestern Mutual Way

The ambition of The Northwestern has been less to be large than to be safe; its aim is to rank first in benefits to policyowners rather than first in size. Valuing quality above quantity, it has preferred to secure its business under certain salutary restrictions and limitations rather than to write a much larger business at the possible sacrifice of those valuable points which have made The Northwestern pre-eminently the policyowner's Company.

Executive Committee • 1888

Exhibit 8. "The Northwestern Mutual Way"

For The Goodyear Tire and Rubber Company for example, the mission statement consists of these four simple words, "Protect Our Good Name." This creed has served as part of Goodyear's heritage since 1915. For over seventy years, it has been the basis for the company's social responsiveness.

Another difference among mission statements is the accessibility of the document. Some companies proudly promulgate their mission statements; others label their mission statements "inside information" and keep them as internal documents.

The purpose of the mission statement also varies from company to company. For some it may simply be written for good public relations. More often, we hope, it will be written because the company has a sincere and honest desire to run its business with sound business principles as stated in the mission statement.

Whatever the reason, many companies put a great deal of time and thought into the drafting of these documents. This is a very expensive process involving not only the expenditure of time, but also risking the reputation of the company. There is a reason that so many companies go through this process.

It would be naïve to believe that all companies follow their corporate philosophy blindly. It would be equally naïve to believe that no company has ever acted contrary to the ideals set forth in their mission statement. Things are rarely that simple.

What is important to consider is the intent of what is stated in the corporate philosophy. The ideals set forth are understandably high. They represent the way the company wants to be viewed, the goals they attempt to achieve. When setting their goals, most companies aim high.

In examining the goals for a company, as set forth in the mission statement, there is one word that is commonly found. That word is "excellence." Many companies aim for excellence in all aspects of their business. They include excellence in products, services, management, integrity, and so on.

Perhaps the word excellence has become something of a buzzword. This may be due to the popularity of several books promoting excellence in business. Whatever the reason, many companies have recognized the importance of striving for excellence. Others still aim to go beyond excellence.

The mission statement may be one way of reinforcing a company's commitment to excellence.

Winn-Dixie Stores, Inc.

Management Objectives [as stated in 1975 annual report]

To operate up to date, clean and conveniently located supermarkets staffed by well trained and courteous personnel, offering customers a complete variety of quality food products at competitive prices.

To deal fairly with customers, employees and suppliers in order to merit their continuing patronage and support.

To operate a financially sound business by energetically increasing sales volume and controlling operating expenses, for the purpose of obtaining a reasonable profit and investment return for shareholders.

To provide employees with the opportunity for training and promotion, while offering them pay, benefits and working conditions equal to or better than those generally available in the food industry in our trade areas.

To offer under our private label program only those items that represent good customer value at reasonable prices.

To innovate and implement better and more efficient ways of serving our customers.

To be a good corporate citizen by complying with all laws regulating Company affairs in keeping with the highest ethical standards.

Exhibit 9. Winn-Dixie Stores' "Management Objectives"

Marion Laboratories: Corporate Missions

- Achieve a performance and people-oriented working environment that stimulates integrity, entrepreneurial spirit, productivity and a sense of responsibility to all Marion associates.
- Achieve positions of market leadership through marketing and distribution of consumable and personal products of integrity and perceived differentiation in selected segments of health care.
- Achieve long-term growth of profits and return on shareholder investment through the management of high risk relative to the external environment.

Exhibit 10. Marion Laboratories' "Corporate Missions"

Rolm Philosophy

ROLM Corporation was founded in 1969 with four goals:

To Make a Profit

To Grow

To Offer Quality Products
   and Customer Support

To Create a Great Place to Work

The four goals are closely interrelated. One cannot exist without the others. In order for ROLM to profit, it must offer quality products and customer support. In order to grow, it must profit. And in order to develop quality products and customer support, ROLM must maintain a work environment conducive to creativity and productivity.

In the course of our history, certain practices have proven successful in achieving the four goals. These practices have become known as the attributes of success at ROLM. The goals and the attributes, taken together, constitute the ROLM philosophy.

ROLM Philosophy provides a bond for this highly decentralized company. We do our best to maintain an entrepreneurial spirit and to avoid bureaucracy through broad decentralization of responsibility and authority. This approach necessarily leads to differences of opinion. However, we believe this is the only environment that provides the individual freedom required for creative thinking and rapid response to the changing needs of the marketplace. We are convinced that a highly structured, bureaucratic organization is much less effective than our organization. Certainly, that form of organization would never attract the excellent people we have at ROLM.

ROLM Philosophy is the basis for most of our decision making. It indicates much of what we are doing at ROLM and where we are headed. This statement of the Philosophy is presented for your consideration and implementation.

President

TO MAKE A PROFIT

A primary reason for the existence of most businesses in our economic society is to make a profit. Making a profit is necessary to finance the business intelligently. On a continuous basis we need additional funds for doing research and development, expanding facilities, upgrading equipment, maintaining inventories, and strengthening sales and service channels. ROLM profits, with the exception of those distributed in our employee profit-sharing plan, have always been totally reinvested in the business.

Further, making a profit is necessary to have the flexibility to make the correct long-term decisions for the company. A consistent profit advance provides a secure basis for thoughtful examination of future possibilities. Undue profit pressure forces an environment in which decisions may be made with poor planning and a short-term view.

TO GROW

A company can compete successfully with others only if it grows. Further, the ultimate reward for our stockholders investment is profitable growth. At ROLM we recognize two other major reasons for steady, planned growth.

First, there is a strategic reason. ROLM competes against the giants of the computer and telecommunications industries. Success in this competition is marked by gaining market share from companies that are less responsive and creative. We must grow to supply these large markets in which we choose to operate.

Secondly, there is a basic human reason for corporate growth. The environment that we continue to create at ROLM is one of expanding opportunity and challenge for our people. The opportunity for the growth of each individual is dependent upon the healthy growth of ROLM Corporation. Conversely, the growth of ROLM Corporation is dependent upon the growth of each individual.

TO OFFER QUALITY PRODUCTS AND CUSTOMER SUPPORT

ROLM has a single basic reason for being in existence: to provide the finest quality products and customer support. We have been and will continue to be distinguished by our excellent products and our efficient customer support.

The goods that go out our back door—our products, our hardware—are conceived and manufactured to be of the highest possible quality. ROLM customers are led to expect the finest. ROLM people are committed to delivering the finest.

However, our products are only a portion of the total quality ROLM offers. We are also committed to providing the best customer support in the industry. This includes: meeting customer needs quickly, interacting with customers professionally, focusing on uptime, and offering a complete range of services. In this manner, we strive to earn the loyalty of our customers.

TO CREATE A GREAT PLACE TO WORK

The first three goals of ROLM are shared by many companies throughout the world. The fourth, "To Create a Great Place to Work," is rare. We know of no other organization that makes this one of its basic goals.

We do this quite simply because we want to attract and motivate the best and the brightest people that we can. In order to attract and motivate the best and the brightest people ROLM promotes a humane and challenging work environment, a very competitive compensation and benefits plan, and physical surroundings befitting the quality of ROLM people.

The humanity and challenge of the ROLM work environment is predicated on a dual responsibility. ROLM Corporation acts to provide equal opportunity to grow and be promoted; fair treatment for each individual; respect for personal privacy; encouragement to succeed; opportunity for creativity; evaluation based on job performance in the context of ROLM Philosophy. ROLM people are expected to respond by being individually accountable; being helpful toward others to enhance teamwork; performing to the best of his/her abilities; and understanding and implementing the ROLM Philosophy.

Exhibit 11. ROLM Corporation's Goals

2

The Missions of History

Mission statements are not unique to corporations. Individuals, institutions, and even governments have documents that embody the spirit of the author and can be considered a form of mission statement. In this chapter we will examine a few missions of groups other than companies.

Perhaps the oldest mission statement can be found in the New Testament of the Bible. It is a commandment given during the Sermon on the Mount and recounted in two places:

> "Therefore all things whatsoever ye would that men should do to you, do ye even so to them: for this is the law and the prophets." (Matthew 7:12)

> "And as ye would that men should do to you, do ye also to them likewise." (Luke 6:31)

The concept presented in these passages is easily recognizable as what is known as the "Golden Rule." Although this idea is very old, it has never lost its appeal. It is the foundation of several of today's major religions, and it is mentioned in some of the mission statements included in this book.

Even here on our own continent mission statements have a long history. They date back as far as the seventeenth century—even before our country was founded. One of the oldest institutions in North America is not a company. Yet it has a mission statement written by its founders to define its purpose. This institution, founded in 1636, had the following as its mission statement:

> To advance learning and to perpetuate it to posterity, dreading to send an illiterate ministry to our churches when our present ministers shall lie in the dust.

This was the mission set forth by the founders of Harvard University. At the time, Harvard was dedicated to teaching the ministry, and they had no competition on this continent. Many things have changed in the three and a half centuries of Harvard's existence. If Harvard were to rewrite its mission statement today to better define its current purpose, there would probably be many changes.

There have been many individuals, too, who have written their own personal creeds, or mission statements. One of the most memorable of these was written by John Davidson Rockefeller, Jr. Although this document was written many years ago, it is still considered by many to be the best personal creed ever written.

There are few names that so appropriately symbolize the "American Dream" as does the name Rockefeller. The mere mention of the name brings thoughts of power and wealth. Mr. Rockefeller was very successful working within the system to build a financial empire. Although he has long since passed away, his words and beliefs live on in his personal creed.

In his creed, Rockefeller speaks of the supreme worth of the individual, thrift, truth, the sacredness of a promise, and so on. They are the thoughts of a man who has been very successful in building an empire for himself and for the generations that have followed him.

Governments, too, have often established mission statements to define their purposes. These can be as simple as a motto, or as complex as the Constitution of the United States. In their advertising, the U.S. Armed Forces state, "We're not a company, we're your country." Like many companies, the United States has a number of documents that could be considered mission statements. In the following pages we will examine two of these as well as missions from other governments.

By taking a brief look back into history, we will find that there are a number of mottoes, slogans, and oaths that resemble mission statements. They have served to define the purpose of the organization that championed them. And they have served as a means of moving people to rally support for the cause and to point them to a common goal. A few of the most recognizable are these:

"*E Pluribus Unum*" Since the Constitution was ratified in 1787, this has become the motto of the United States. Literally meaning, "Out of many, one," this represents the goal of this country: to unite the diversity of ethnic groups and interests into a nation with a shared identity.

"*Liberté! Egalité! Fraternité!*" This phrase, meaning "Liberty! Equality! Fraternity!" served as the motto of the French Revolution in 1789. The French revolutionaries rallied around this motto, fighting to achieve these objectives.

"*A Mari Usque ad Mare*" This phrase, which translated means "From Sea to Sea," has served as the national motto of Canada since 1867, when Canada achieved independence as a result of the British North America Act. Similar to the national motto of the United States, this phrase represents the goal of uniting many diverse ethnic groups into a single nation with a shared identity.

The Creed

—I believe in the supreme worth of the individual and in his right to life, liberty, and the pursuit of happiness.

—I believe that every right implies a responsibility; every opportunity, an obligation; every possession, a duty.

—I believe that the law was made for man and not man for the law; that government is the servant of the people and not their master.

—I believe in the dignity of labor, whether with head or hand; that the world owes no man a living, but owes every man an opportunity to make a living.

—I believe that thrift is essential to well-ordered living and that economy is a prime requisite of a sound financial structure, whether in government, business, or personal affairs.

—I believe that truth and justice are fundamental to an enduring social order.

—I believe in the sacredness of a promise, that a man's word should be as good as his bond; that character—not wealth or power or position—is of supreme worth.

—I believe that rendering of useful service is the common duty of mankind and that only in the purifying fire of sacrifice is the dross of selfishness consumed and the greatness of the human soul set free.

—I believe in an all-wise and all-loving God, named by whatever name, and that the individual's highest fulfillment, greatest happiness, and widest usefulness are to be found in living in harmony with His will.

—I believe that love is the greatest thing in the world; that it alone can overcome hate; that right can and will triumph over might.

Exhibit 12. J. D. Rockefeller, Creed

Each of the above sentiments is, in a sense, a mission statement. Each reflects beliefs for which the people were willing to fight, and in some cases to die. They are admirable goals the people of these nations set out to achieve.

In addition to the U.S. national motto, there is a second document that can be considered the mission statement of the United States. It is the Constitution, which was ratified by a convention of the States on September 17, 1787. Although the Constitution has changed over the years, it has served us in guiding our country for over two hundred years. The goal of the Constitution is stated in its Preamble:

> We, the people of the United States, in order to form a more perfect Union, establish justice, insure domestic tranquility, provide for the common defense, promote the general welfare, and secure the blessings of liberty to ourselves and our posterity, do ordain and establish this Constitution for the United States of America.

The Constitution originally consisted of the Preamble and seven Articles. All thirteen of the colonies embraced this document before December of 1791 when the first ten amendments, the Bill of Rights, were declared in force. A fourteenth state, Vermont, adopted the Constitution more than a month before it was admitted into the Union.

To allow the document to evolve and keep pace with the changing times, the Constitution had its own provisions for adding amendments. In the two hundred years that the Constitution has been in force, twenty-four amendments have been added, while only one (the eighteenth) has been repealed.

Like the federal government, many of our states have adopted mottoes. In fact forty-nine of the fifty states have official mottoes. Just as departments of companies work together to achieve a total company identity, so too, do the mottoes of states add together to form our country's identity. Each state motto tells a little about the character of the state and the beliefs of their people.

It is interesting to look at the motto of each state and compare it to the era in which the state entered the union. By doing so, we can get an understanding of the importance of the motto to the people of the state.

The mottoes of the original thirteen colonies were similar in spirit to that of the Revolutionary War era. They show an enthusiasm for those tenets which built this country: "Liberty and Justice" (Delaware), and "By the Sword She Seeks Peace, but Peace Only Under Liberty" (Massachusetts). And they show a willingness to fight for these tenets: "Live Free or Die" (New Hampshire).

Some of the mottoes of states admitted to the Union during later times of peace speak not of positive personal attributes, nor of the defending of rights. Rather they serve to describe physical attributes of those states: "If You Seek a Pleasant Peninsula, Look About You" (Michigan), "The Crossroads of America" (Indiana), and "The Star of the North" (Minnesota).

The largest state, Alaska, is one of the most beautiful and abundant in natural resources. Yet this is the only state that has not adopted an official motto.

Unlike other mission statements, the motto of a state rarely changes. Once written a state's motto will endure. Perhaps this is one reason why the motto tends to reflect the spirit of the people at the time the state entered the union. The states' mottoes also tend to reflect enduring goals such as equality, peace, tranquility, freedom, and so on. This is a second reason that there is no need to revise a state's motto.

In the preceding we can see two things that are readily apparent. First of all, the idea of having a mission statement is not new. It is an idea that has a long history both in this country and throughout the world. Additionally, missions are not unique to corporations. There are many mission statements written for institutions, governments, and individuals.

Given the history and the wide exposure of mission statements, it is likely that they will continue to exist as long as there are people who champion them.

State Mottoes

ALABAMA (1819)	We dare defend our rights
ALASKA (1959)	No motto
ARIZONA (1912)	Didat Deus (God enriches)
ARKANSAS (1836)	Regnat Populus (Let the people rule)
CALIFORNIA (1850)	Eureka (I have found it)
COLORADO (1876)	Nil sine numine (Nothing without God)
*CONNECTICUT (1788)	Qui transtulit sustinet (He who is transplanted sustains)
*DELAWARE (1787)	Liberty and independence
FLORIDA (1845)	In God we trust

*GEORGIA (1788)	Wisdom, justice, moderation
HAWAII (1960)	Righteousness perpetuates the life of the land
IDAHO (1890)	Esto perpetua (Exist forever)
ILLINOIS (1818)	State sovereignty, national union
INDIANA (1816)	The crossroads of America
IOWA (1846)	Our liberties we prize and our rights we will maintain
KANSAS (1861)	Ad astra per aspera (To the stars through difficulties)
KENTUCKY (1792)	United we stand, divided we fall
LOUISIANA (1812)	Union, justice, confidence
MAINE (1820)	Dirigo (I guide)
*MARYLAND (1788)	Fatti mascchili, parole femine (Manly deeds, womanly words)
*MASSACHUSETTS (1788)	Ense petit placidam sub libertate quitem (By the sword she seeks peace, but peace only under liberty)
MICHIGAN (1837)	Si quaeris peninsulam amoenam circumspice (If you seek a pleasant peninsula, look about you)
MINNESOTA (1858)	L'Etoile du nord (The star of the north)
MISSISSIPPI (1817)	Virtute et armis (By valor and arms)
MISSOURI (1821)	Salus populi suprema lex esto (Welfare of the people shall be the supreme law)
MONTANA (1889)	Oro y plata (Gold and silver)
NEBRASKA (1867)	Equality before the law
NEVADA (1864)	All for our country
*NEW HAMPSHIRE (1788)	Live free or die
*NEW JERSEY (1787)	Liberty and prosperity
NEW MEXICO (1912)	Crescit eundo (It grows as it goes)
*NEW YORK (1788)	Excelsior (Higher, always upward)
*NORTH CAROLINA (1789)	Esse quam videri (To be, rather than to seem)
NORTH DAKOTA (1889)	Liberty and union, now and forever, one and inseparable
OHIO (1803)	With God all things are possible

OKLAHOMA (1907)	Labor omnia vincit (Labor conquers all things)
OREGON (1859)	The union
*PENNSYLVANIA (1787)	Virtue, liberty and independence
*RHODE ISLAND (1790)	Hope
*SOUTH CAROLINA (1788)	Dum spiro spero (While I breathe, I hope)
SOUTH DAKOTA (1889)	Under God, the people rule
TENNESSEE (1796)	Agriculture, commerce
TEXAS (1845)	Friendship
UTAH (1896)	Industry
VERMONT (1791)	Freedom and unity
*VIRGINIA (1788)	Sic semper tyrannis (Thus always to tyrants)
WASHINGTON (1889)	Ai-Ki (By and by)
WEST VIRGINIA (1863)	Montani semper liberi (Mountaineers always free)
WISCONSIN (1848)	Forward
WYOMING (1890)	Cedant arma togae (Let arms yield to the gown)

*Original thirteen colonies
Year in parentheses is the year the state entered the union.

Exhibit 13. Mottoes of the Fifty States

3

A Corporate
Philosophy on Trial

Mary Kellerman, a twelve-year-old girl from the Chicago area, died on September 28, 1982.

A few miles away, Adam Janus collapsed in his home. Paramedics could not revive him.

Later that evening, Stanley Janus, the brother of Adam Janus, also died.

A few hours later, Stanley's wife Theresa was admitted to the hospital. She survived for two days and then died.

Before the weekend three others, all from the Chicago area, joined them in death.

These seven deaths were sudden and unexpected. Initially, the causes of death were thought to range from stroke to massive heart attack. But when three members of the same family were admitted to the hospital, Dr. Kim at Northwest Community Hospital grew suspicious. All had dilated pupils and low blood pressure.

Dr. Kim called the Rocky Mountain Poison Center to discuss the symptoms with Dr. John Sullivan. After discussing the case, Dr. Sullivan narrowed the possibilities to two.

When the first possibility, hydrogen sulphide gas was ruled out, there was only one thing left: the seven must have died from cyanide poisoning.

Blood samples taken from the victims confirmed the theory. The levels of cyanide in each of the victims was tremendously high.

Perhaps it was through sheer luck that the source of the cyanide poisoning was discovered. Two firefighters, Phillip Cappiteel and Richard Keyworth made the discovery. All of the victims had taken Extra Strength TYLENOL® capsules shortly before dying. It was just a guess, when Keyworth said that the TYLENOL® might have been the source of the poison.

A massive campaign began to alert the public. Children were sent home from schools with notes about the poisonings. Boy Scouts went door to door spreading the news. Police drove through the streets shouting over bullhorns. Church groups organized telephone campaigns.

Once the link was made, there was a lot of pressure to make some very difficult decisions. McNeil Consumer Products (the maker of TYLENOL®), and Johnson & Johnson (McNeil's parent company) had to react quickly and effectively to prevent the occurrence of future deaths.

TYLENOL® was the largest revenue-producing product for Johnson & Johnson. It was marketed to help reduce pain. Unfortunately, now it was associated with death.

The cause of the poisonings had yet to be determined. The possibilities were many. It could have been a random poisoning. It could have been industrial sabotage. Or it could have been a critical mistake in the manufacturing process. Whatever the cause, however, there was no time to delay. Some very difficult decisions had to be made.

Johnson & Johnson acted quickly. It ordered the immediate recall of Extra Strength TYLENOL® capsules. It sent out approximately 450,000 electronic messages to the medical community. It posted a $100,000 reward for help in finding the murderer. It did everything in its power to warn the public about the problem.

The company also agreed to cooperate fully with the press. It opened its doors to the press and answered as many questions as it could. As the facts were uncovered, the press was informed.

Throughout the entire crisis, Johnson & Johnson did something extraordinary for a multimillion dollar company: it put the safety of the public first and its own profits second. It did this despite the fact that it was also a victim of the attack.

Another thing that was extraordinary about this incident was the reaction of the press. There were opportunities for the press to overreact and to blame the situation on Johnson & Johnson. Yet throughout the crisis, the press acted responsibly.

Often during times of crisis, the press is accused of being overzealous. They are accused of being insensitive to companys' positions and of sensationalizing the facts.

Such was not the case in this instance. Throughout the entire crisis, the press praised Johnson & Johnson for its reaction to the poisonings. The coverage was overwhelmingly positive. A sampling of the opinions expressed in newspapers across the country show nearly universal support for how the company dealt with the crisis:

San Antonio, Texas *Express and News*: "In spite of the $100 million loss it was facing, the company . . . never put its interests ahead of solving the murders and protecting the public. Such corporate responsibility deserves support."

Wall Street Journal: "Johnson & Johnson, the parent company that makes TYLENOL®, set the pattern of industry response. Without being asked, it quickly withdrew Extra-Strength TYLENOL® from the market at a very considerable expense. . . . The company chose to take a large loss rather than expose anyone to further risk."*

Washington Post: "Though the hysteria and frustration generated by random murder have often obscured the company's actions, Johnson & Johnson has effectively demonstrated how a major business ought to handle a disaster. . . . From the day the deaths were linked to the poisoned TYLENOL® . . . Johnson & Johnson has succeeded in portraying itself to the public as a company willing to do what's right regardless of cost."

St. Petersburg, Florida *Evening Independent*: "The company has been straight-forward and honest since the first news of the possible TYLENOL® link in the Chicago-area deaths. Some firms would have tried to cover up, lie, or say 'no comment.' Johnson & Johnson knows better. Its first concern was to safeguard the public from further contamination, and the best way to do that was to let people know what had occurred by speaking frankly with the news media."

It is rare to see such universal agreement from the press, and even rarer still when there is so much at stake. More often there is a great deal of second guessing, and the victim company is prey to undue criticism.

The press was not alone in supporting Johnson & Johnson for its actions. Less than one month after the poisonings, the FDA gave Johnson & Johnson a "clean bill of health" concluding that the tampering of TYLENOL® had occurred somewhere in the distribution cycle. The commissioner of the FDA, Dr. Arthur H. Hayes, began making public service announcements alerting the public that Johnson & Johnson was the innocent victim of this attack.

But perhaps the most important vote of confidence came not from the press, nor from the government. The most important vote of confidence came from the public. It did this by continuing to purchase Extra Strength TYLENOL® capsules. Within months, the company had regained 98 percent of the market share that it had the day of the poisoning.

What could have destroyed the company turned out to be only a trial for the pharmaceutical giant. Johnson & Johnson did more than survive the crisis, they flourished. They turned the tragedy of the TYLENOL® poisonings into a marketing triumph.

---

*Reprinted by permission of *The Wall Street Journal*, © Dow Jones and Company, Inc. 1988. All rights reserved.

Apparently there is universal agreement that Johnson & Johnson responded in the best manner possible. The decisions, which were made quickly, turned out to be made in the best interest of everyone involved: the company, the public, the government, and the press.

To what does the company attribute this vote of confidence? What is it that made Johnson & Johnson act the way it did?

The management of Johnson & Johnson attributed the success to its corporate mission statement. The quotes reprinted below show that the company's management philosophy entitled "Our Credo" was a valuable guide in the decision process:

> " . . . the events surrounding the TYLENOL® crisis were so atypical that we found ourselves improvising every step of the way. I doubt that even now we could devise a plan of action to deal with all aspects of the TYLENOL® situation. Events happened so quickly and so unpredictably that it would be impossible to anticipate the critical decisions that had to be made. Crisis planning did not see us through this tragedy nearly as much as the sound business management philosophy that is embodied in our Credo. It was the Credo that prompted the decisions that enabled us to make the right early decisions that eventually led to the comeback phase." (David Clare, president of Johnson & Johnson)

> "[The crisis] required literally dozens of people to make hundreds of decisions in painfully short periods of time. Even when we had time for careful consideration, most of the decisions were complicated, involving considerable risk. And we had no historical precedent to rely on . . . the guidance of the Credo played the single most important role in our decision making. . . . The Credo was tested—and it worked." (James Burke, chairman of Johnson & Johnson)

Those people closest to the crisis credited the Credo for helping them make decisions. When there was no time for weighing all of the options, they had to rely on their company philosophy. And they were not disappointed.

"The Credo" has been a part of Johnson & Johnson's heritage for many years. It was written shortly after World War II. The author, General Robert Wood Johnson, was a young brigadier general who had served in Washington as head of the Small War Plants Board. As part of the preamble to this document, General Johnson stated:

> Institutions, both public and private, exist because the people want them, believe in them, or at least are willing to tolerate them. The day has passed when business was a private matter—if it ever really

Our Credo

We believe our first responsibility is to the doctors, nurses and patients,
to mothers and all others who use our products and services.
In meeting their needs everything we do must be of high quality.
We must constantly strive to reduce our costs
in order to maintain reasonable prices.
Customers' orders must be serviced promptly and accurately.
Our suppliers and distributors must have an opportunity
to make a fair profit.

We are responsible to our employees,
the men and women who work with us throughout the world.
Everyone must be considered as an individual.
We must respect their dignity and recognize their merit.
They must have a sense of security in their jobs.
Compensation must be fair and adequate,
and working conditions clean, orderly and safe.
Employees must feel free to make suggestions and complaints.
There must be equal opportunity for employment, development
and advancement for those qualified.
We must provide competent management,
and their actions must be just and ethical.

We are responsible to the communities in which we live and work
and to the world community as well.
We must be good citizens — support good works and charities
and bear our fair share of taxes.
We must encourage civic improvements and better health and education.
We must maintain in good order
the property we are privileged to use,
protecting the environment and natural resources.

Our final responsibility is to our stockholders.
Business must make a sound profit.
We must experiment with new ideas.
Research must be carried on, innovative programs developed
and mistakes paid for.
New equipment must be purchased, new facilities provided
and new products launched.
Reserves must be created to provide for adverse times.
When we operate according to these principles,
the stockholders should realize a fair return.

Johnson & Johnson

Exhibit 14. Johnson & Johnson's "Our Credo"

was. In a business society, every act of business has social con-
sequences and may arouse public interest. Every time business
hires, builds, sells or buys, it is acting for the people as well as for
itself, and it must accept full responsibility for its acts.

General Johnson could never have imagined that the Credo would be
tested to such a great extent. Nor could he have imagined that the document
would come to mean so much to the company. Yet these words he wrote,
helped see the company through what could have been the company's
greatest tragedy.

Over the years, the Credo has changed. Some of the words remain the
same, while others have been changed substantively. Still others have simply been modernized. Some of the responsibilities have been expanded
because the world has become more complicated. Despite the changes,
however, the basic philosophy has remained unchanged.

The Credo articulates a number of responsibilities the company has to
those who share a business relationship. The responsibilities include the
customer, the employees, the communities, and finally the stockholder.
These guidelines have been a part of Johnson & Johnson's heritage since
they were presented to the employees in 1947.

The company's priorities are specifically outlined in the Credo. It points
out that the company considers the customer its first priority, and profits
its last. The following statements, quoted directly from the Credo, illustrate
this point:

> We believe our first responsibility is to the doctors, nurses and
> patients, to mothers and all others who use our products and ser-
> vices. . . .

> Our final responsibility is to our stockholders. Business must make
> a sound profit.

Given the priorities as expressed in the Credo, Johnson & Johnson had
little choice but to act as it did. The result of doing so, speaks for itself.

We will never know for sure if Johnson & Johnson would have handled
things differently without the Credo. We will never know if there would
be such universal support for their actions. But to Johnson & Johnson, the
Credo played the most vital role in helping to guide decisions during the
greatest crisis in its corporate history.

4

Is There a Need for a Mission Statement?

As we have seen, "Our Credo" played a valuable role in helping Johnson & Johnson deal with the TYLENOL® crisis. But Johnson & Johnson is by no means unique for having a written company philosophy. There are many companies that have similar documents. Sometimes these documents are available for public inspection and other times they are held as confidential. But few, if any, have been tested to the extent of Johnson & Johnson's Credo.

The titles of the mission statements are quite varied. They include "corporate philosophy," "objectives," "credo," "our way," and so on. But despite the variety of names, the idea is the same: to define what is important to the company.

Not everyone is convinced of the value of having a written mission statement. While some think they are vital, others feel that they are of little value. But despite the disagreement, it may be interesting to evaluate some comments of corporate executives regarding the need and value of mission statements.

The following is a sampling of comments about mission statements. Some are positive, and others are negative, but all provide insight about their value.

> "I have seen public 'mission statements' of a number of corporations, mostly as they appear in their annual reports and I must admit I am not terribly impressed with these. In fact, I do not remember even one that was sufficiently impressive to recommend to you for reading! Mostly, the ones I have seen are of the Pablum school . . . being for motherhood, the flag, ethical dealings with the public, etc. . . . things which any prudent person would expect should be so much a part of a company that they could reasonably

be taken for granted without having to be articulated." (Dorothy Lorant, vice president for public relations and advertising, The Greyhound Corporation)

"All of our corporate policy flows from these principles." (Joseph F. Awad, corporate director, Reynolds Aluminum)

"This code, which was originally adopted in the mid–1970's and has been updated periodically, has been distributed to all Dow Corning employees worldwide to assure that its' principles remain a fundamental part of our Corporate culture. It has also been distributed widely to customers, suppliers, consultants, government officials and other relevant parties. It has been produced in a wide variety of foreign languages for use in key countries around the world. . . . I'm sure you'll see why Dow Corning is proud, not only of this document, but more basically of the philosophy it describes." (Edward Steinhoff, vice president, Dow Corning Corporation)

"If a corporation is to succeed and experience continuing, long-term growth, there must exist a meaningful company philosophy that justifies the personal commitment and dedication of its people." (Jack J. Crocker, Super Valu Stores, Inc.)

"We take very seriously the idea that a good company should focus itself around a central concept of its contribution to society." (Joseph T. Stewart, Jr., senior vice president, corporate affairs, Squibb Corporation)

"No matter how responsibly a corporation behaves, it will be viewed with skepticism unless it effectively communicates its activities, its plans, and its goals to its many publics. This then is the final obligation, and perhaps the most important of all." (J. Peter Grace, chairman of the board, W. R. Grace & Company)

"The objectives set forth are more than just words in our company—they describe the guidelines by which we strive to manage." (J. Alec Reinhardt, vice president, finance, Cooper Tire & Rubber Co.)

" . . . we prefer to demonstrate our corporate commitment to society through our many responsible actions which are substantial and wide ranging, rather than talking about them in a glossy brochure." (James F. Kostecky, director, corporate support programs, Bethlehem Steel Corporation)

"Each of us can reflect credit upon the Company as a whole by keeping them [Texaco's Guiding Principles and Objectives] foremost in our mind when carrying out our duties and responsibilities." (John K. McKinley, former chairman of the board and chief executive officer, Texaco, Inc.)

It is quite apparent that there is no universal agreement on the value of a mission statement. While some feel they are important and swear by them, others are not convinced. Some think they embody the corporation's philosophy, and others feel they contain nothing more than common sense. However, in spite of the controversy, much can be learned by careful examination of these documents.

Despite the disagreement about the need for mission statements, the companies who have adopted them almost universally embrace them. One such company is Armstrong. In its "Principles and Objectives," Armstrong has this to say: "We firmly believe that the most significant factor contributing to the Company's progress has been the strict adherence to sound principles—principles laid down by the founder and carried forward and given new dimensions by succeeding managements."

The purpose of this book is not to evaluate the need for a mission statement, nor is it to subjectively criticize the values of a given company, or to judge whether or not a company lives up to its written proclamation. The purpose of this book is to look at mission statements—to see what they have in common and to see how they contrast. In evaluating these documents, there will be no attempt to judge whether or not a given company lives up to its philosophy. There will be no attempt to compare a company's actions with its philosophy. Rather, we will look only at what the documents say.

As stated earlier, the true test of any company is not in what it says but rather in what it does. The true test is not in how a company views itself, it is in how it is viewed by its many publics.

Companies exist for a variety of reasons. Some simply want to earn a profit. Still others want to fulfill a need. Others want to provide a service. Whatever the purpose, the company must be successful in fulfilling a need if it is to survive.

5

Making a Mission Statement

The mission statement is a document that tells a little bit about the character of the company. It is a reflection of the company's personality. It is a document that points out the company's priorities as determined by the key members of the management.

Because of this, the mission statement gives insight into the thoughts of those people who are charged with determining the company's future. The words must be carefully chosen so that there is little chance of misinterpretation.

The mission statement can do a number of different things. It may point the direction in which the company intends to go, or it may define the market which the company hopes to service. It can set the priorities held by the company's management, or it can do all of these things. But whatever the intent of the mission statement, a great deal of care is taken when committing the company mission statement to writing.

The mission statement is a reflection on the company. It will be read and evaluated by many of those who see it. Often it will be criticized. Perhaps this is because there seems to be a great deal of skepticism about the mission statement. Good intentions, no matter how firmly held, are often mistrusted.

For many, it is easy to read a mission statement and be unimpressed. It's easy to say that a mission statement is nothing more than common sense. It is true that a substantial number of ideas in mission statements are just that. It is equally true, however, that common sense often can be easily overlooked.

Because all businesses are made up of people, the human element can never be eliminated. Ultimately, all decisions are made by people. And those decisions are based on facts and the interpretation of those facts.

To illustrate, consider these points. Many companies have failed because they have forgotten to consider the needs of their customers. Other com-

⬛ii SMITH INTERNATIONAL, INC.
PHILOSOPHY

Committing ourselves to integrity, it is our purpose to:

1. Earn the respect, confidence and loyalty of **OUR CUSTOMERS** by serving them so well that they profit from their association with us.

2. Provide **OUR PEOPLE** the highest degree of opportunity and challenge for the realization of their ambitions in terms of career, rewards and family security.

3. Fulfill our obligations to **OUR INVESTORS** to such an extent that they are both proud and anxious to share in our enterprise.

4. Be fair and courteous with **OUR SUPPLIERS** to encourage their contributions to our success.

5. Not malign **OUR COMPETITORS** and to gain their respect by ethical practices in our own business.

6. Be good citizens of **OUR COMMUNITIES.**

7. Actively participate in **OUR GOVERNMENTAL PROGRAMS** where we believe them to be consistent, in the long term, with the philosophy stated here — and more particularly those programs related to energy conservation and the environment.

Jerry W. Neely
Jerry W. Neely
Chairman & Chief
Executive Officer

Exhibit 15. Smith International's "Philosophy"

Styrotech Corporation
Our Business Principles

PEOPLE

The employees of Styrotech Corporation are our greatest asset. They must feel secure, challenged, and in control of their own destiny. They must feel confident in their leadership, and strive for common goals. Each employee must believe that he/she is treated fairly and with integrity. All lines of communication must be open in all directions and levels of authority.

PRINCIPLES

The management of Styrotech Corporation must always seek the principles involved in any question or evaluation. All decisions must be based on full facts and awareness.

THE CUSTOMER

Our company exists primarily to serve the customer. Our mission is to manufacture the highest quality products at the lowest possible price. By achieving this, the needs of the customers, employees, and the shareholders will be satisfied.

SIMPLICITY

Simplicity in policy, principle, product design, buildings, manufacturing areas, personnel policies, and management structure will lead to a very productive organization and a successful business.

COMPETITION

We believe that a healthy competition is helpful to a successful long term business.

Exhibit 16. Styrotech Corporation's "Our Business Principles"

panies have suffered huge financial losses from lawsuits because they have knowingly and deliberately put the public at risk. And finally, some companies have tried to cover up the facts when some negative information has come to light about their products.

Listening to the customer may be nothing more than common sense, and yet it is often overlooked. Making public safety a high priority may be common sense, and yet it too can be forgotten. Honestly dealing with problems may be common sense, and yet it is very difficult. More often than not, it is the company that pays attention to these kinds of details that will be one of the most highly regarded and successful companies.

A mission statement may do little more than remind people of the basic principles of good business. In doing so, it provides a yardstick by which to measure their actions. While it is easy to get caught up in day-to-day activities, it is often very valuable to be reminded of basic principles of good business and common sense. A carefully worded mission statement can do this.

There is often a great deal of skepticism regarding the honest intents of mission statements. Therefore, the words must be very carefully chosen. By failing to carefully select the words, a company leaves itself wide open for undue criticism. Perhaps it is from envy, or possibly mistrust, but there

---

Varian Associates, Inc.
Basic Corporate Objectives

PROFITABILITY

Objective: To produce a level of profitability that allows steady corporate growth and provides the financial basis required to attain all corporate objectives.

CUSTOMER SATISFACTION

Objective: To serve our world-wide markets with products and services that satisfy customer needs and are of exceptional quality, reliability and value.

FIELDS OF INTEREST

Objective: To serve our diverse markets in an outstanding manner. To seek significant new related areas of opportunity where our ideas, technology, marketing, and manufacturing skills appropriately combine to offer real value to the market and satisfactory financial return to the corporation. Our primary focus remains on those markets and market segments where our capabilities permit us to attain a leadership position with favorable differentiation from competing products.

SOUND GROWTH

Objective: To grow at a rate made possible by our creativity in identifying new market opportunities, and by our capabilities—in both new and existing markets—for developing, marketing, manufacturing, and financing the products which meet market needs.

WORK ENVIRONMENT

Objective: To maintain a satisfying work environment that promotes creativity, initiative, productivity, and cooperation; an environment that allows Varian to attract, hold, motivate, and reward people of exceptional ability in an atmosphere of integrity and concern for the individual.

RESPONSIBLE OWNERSHIP

Objective: To be a good corporate citizen in those communities and countries where we operate, including the selective contribution of human, financial, or other corporate resources, where appropriate.

Exhibit 17. Varian Associate's "Basic Corporate Objectives"

---

is a tendency not to believe in the integrity of the intent of large companies.

Mission statements take on a variety of forms and lengths. They can be as simple as a single sentence, or they can go on for pages. They may concentrate on only one trait, or they may stress many. But each mission statement has a personality which is unique and reflective of the individual ideals of the corporate directors.

Although there are differences in the mission statements of various companies, there are also many similarities. In most mission statements, there are several elements that are repeated over and over again. These include things such as a dedication to the employees, the profit motive, the customer, a commitment to quality, and a responsibility to the community. Each of these will be discussed below and in the succeeding chapters.

It would be impossible to select one single aspect that is the top priority for all companies. Each company sets its own priorities. The top priority for one company may have a lower priority for another company. Despite this fact there are several conclusions to be drawn about companies and how their priorities are reflected in their mission statements.

More companies choose the employee as the highest priority. Perhaps this is not surprising when you consider the fact that companies often spend more on their employees than on any other single asset. Often it is the employee that can make or break the success of a company.

Many corporations feel they have an obligation to their employees. They believe they have an obligation to help each of their employees to develop to his or her greatest potential. It is in the best interest of both the employee and the company to achieve this goal. The success of both the employee and the company goes hand in hand.

It is also in the best interest of the company to keep the employee as happy as possible in terms of career. Only by keeping the employees reasonably happy can the company be assured of keeping their employees. All things considered if an employee would be happier working somewhere else, what incentive would he or she have to stay with the current job?

As corporations have an obligation to the employees, many believe that the employees have a reciprocal obligation to the company. This obligation may include such things as loyalty to the company, providing the company with an honest day's work for an honest day's pay, and ethical conduct on and off the job.

A second high priority for many companies and their mission statements is the profit objective. This too is to be expected because profits are the basis of the free-enterprise system. Profits measure how well a company is performing. A company that cannot produce a profit cannot continue to exist for a prolonged period of time. Even those companies considered non profit must at least live within monetary constraints or perish.

Profits serve as a measure of how well a company operates. A highly profitable company is a highly successful company. Both short- and long-term profits demonstrate the ability of the corporation to meet the needs of society. The company that fails to produce a profit, will eventually fail.

A third obligation for a company is to its stockholders, the owners of the company. By investing their money, the stockholders have entrusted their money to the corporation. It is therefore a responsibility of the company to serve as guardian of that investment and to help maximize the return to the stockholder by maximizing the profits.

Another element commonly found in mission statements is the goal to meet the needs of the customer. Customer satisfaction is a central goal of many companies because it is the customer who ultimately determines the success or failure of any company. With every dollar spent, the customer shows approval for, or disapproval of, the company.

For many companies, customer satisfaction can only be achieved through producing a product of high quality. This commitment to quality is another

Dennison
Corporate Philosophies

EMPLOYEES

Every employee is entitled to a decent wage consistent with his contribution and the cost of living in his area.

Every employee is entitled to a decent benefit package that will provide for him when he cannot provide for himself and his family through no fault of his own.

Every employee is entitled to a share of the profits above an adequate return to the shareholders and the needs of the business.

Every employee is entitled to a piece of the wealth he creates through his receiving a portion of the equity.

CUSTOMERS

Every customer is entitled to the timely receipt of the product or service he buys from us at a fair price.

Every customer is entitled to receive the quality level he requested or that which is consistent with what we ourselves would expect to receive.

Every customer is entitled to receive a safe product that will not maim or injure him.

COMMUNITIES

Every community in which we do business is entitled to expect that we will conduct our business in a neat premise that does not pollute the air, water or land nearby.

Every community in which we do business is entitled to expect that we will conduct our business in a way that is consistent with high ethical standards and local laws.

SHAREHOLDERS

Every shareholder is entitled to receive a maximum return on his investment consistent with, but not superior to, our responsibilities to employees, customers and the communities where we do business.

Exhibit 18. Dennison's "Corporate Philosophies"

element common to mission statements. By committing itself to quality, the company hopes to achieve a broad base of customers. A customer's needs can be best satisfied by providing good quality and value in the products manufactured. Since most companies rely on repeated customer purchases, the commitment to quality is of paramount importance.

Yet another element common to mission statements is the idea of being a responsible member of the community. A corporation is a member of the community in which it operates. It draws employees and customers from that community. Many corporations express a commitment to return something to that community through charitable contributions, political support, and responsible action.

Another part of its being a part of the community involves its responsibility to protect natural resources. This includes the wise use of these resources and the protection of the environment from pollutants.

A final element of mission statements is the mention of positive personality traits which are beneficial to both the company and the employees. These include such things as integrity, trust, high ethical standards, belief in oneself, teamwork, religious belief, and honesty. These personality traits help the mission statement itself to develop a personality of its own.

Together these are the elements common to mission statements. They include the basic elements of good business—dedication to employees, the profit motive, the customer, the community, quality and excellence, and positive personality traits.

Although each of these elements is listed separately, they all must go hand in hand. For example, profits cannot be achieved without a high degree of customer satisfaction. Quality cannot be achieved without the dedication of good employees. There must be a proper balance of all priorities. The company that can achieve the best balance will, in the long run, be the most successful company.

Corning Today... and Tomorrow

One requirement of change is understanding who we are and where we want to go.

OUR PURPOSE

We are dedicated to the total success of Corning Glass Works as a worldwide competitor.

We Choose to compete in four broad business sectors.

One is Specialty Glass and Ceramics, our historical base, where our technical skills will continue to drive the development of an ever-broadening range of products for diverse applications. The other three are Consumer Housewares, Laboratory Sciences, and Telecommunications. Here we will build on existing strengths, and the needs of the markets we serve will dictate the technologies we use and the range of products and services we provide.

Our commitment is to provide superior long-range economic benefits to our customers, our employees, our shareholders, and the communities in which we operate.

OUR VALUES

We have a set of enduring beliefs that are engrained in the way we think and act. These values guide our choices, defining for us the right course of action, the clearest direction, the preferred response. Consistent with these values we set our objectives, formulate our strategies, and judge our results. Only by living these values will we achieve our purpose.

QUALITY
INTEGRITY
PERFORMANCE
LEADERSHIP
TECHNOLOGY
INDEPENDENCE
THE INDIVIDUAL

Quality We insist that Total Quality be the guiding principle of our business life. This means new ways of working together. It means knowing and meeting the requirements of our customers and our co-workers. It means doing it right the first time, on time, every time.

Integrity We demand honesty, decency, fairness. Respect must characterize all of our internal and external relationships.

Performance We hold ourselves and each other, as individuals and as an organization, accountable for our results.

Leadership We are a leader, not a follower. This extends to the markets we serve, our multiple technologies, our manufacturing processes, our management practices, and our financial performance. The goods and services we produce must never be ordinary and must always be truly useful.

Technology We lead primarily by technical innovation. This belief in the power of technology is common to all our parts. It is the glue that binds us together. We are committed to translating our specific expertise into goods and services, to expanding the range of our scientific competence, and to linking these abilities with new market needs.

Independence We cherish our corporate freedom. This condition has fostered the innovation and initiative that makes our company great.

The Individual We know in the end that the commitment and contribution of all employees will determine our success. Open relationships with each other, and with our customers, are essential. Therefore, each employee must have the opportunity to participate fully, to grow professionally, and to develop to his or her highest potential.

OPERATING PRINCIPLES

We will maintain a system of Total Quality management throughout the company.

We will know the requirements for leadership in all of our important businesses, markets and technologies; and we will operate and invest to meet those requirements.

We will maintain management, personnel evaluation, and financial reward systems which encourage entrepreneurial risk taking and high achievement.

We will decentralize wherever appropriate to put the power of decision in the hands of those closest to our customers.

We will maintain a system of strategic planning, management information, and controls which is detailed enough to allow management at all levels to exercise their responsibilities, but which is not unnecessarily burdensome.

We will pursue conservative but flexible financial policies in order to ensure our independence, our survival in any sustained economic difficulties, and our ability to respond quickly to business opportunities.

We will manage our assets to get maximum productivity from every dollar of invested capital.

We will manufacture our products and provide our services in locations that offer long-term competitive advantage.

We will manage our businesses and choose our investments to obtain the greatest possible assurance of employment security for all our employees.

We will continue to view joint ventures and acquisitions as appropriate vehicles to capitalize more quickly and fully on new technologies and market opportunities.

We will listen to our employees and gain the full benefit of their knowledge and experience; and we will discuss with them our beliefs, our plans, our expectations, and our hopes.

Exhibit 19. Corning Glass Works' "Corning Today...and Tomorrow"

Statement of Purpose

PREAMBLE

This Statement of Purpose exists to define the fundamental beliefs of ESI. We intend to manage the company in keeping with these beliefs.

One of the most important commitments we have made is to the concept of partnership. We believe this is the best way to work with all those who have a stake in ESI's success—our customers, employees, shareholders and suppliers•

OUR CUSTOMERS

Customer satisfaction is what keeps us in business and makes growth possible. "Value" is the key—a concept that includes not only product usefulness and quality, but also price and performance, and partnership.

We believe in providing unmatched value. That's accomplished by meeting our customer's needs better than anyone else.

We must be customer oriented in all we do. Every job at ESI exists to satisfy our customer's needs. We do this by developing, producing or supporting products and services for our customers.

Our products will be judged in terms of our ability to meet our customer's need for innovation, quality and reliability. By meeting those needs we are giving our customers real value. Leadership in our markets demands that we anticipate the ever-changing needs of our customers and meet those needs with a continual flow of new and superior products and services•

OUR PEOPLE

ESI's greatest resource is the individual and collective potential of our people. We believe one of our critical responsibilities is to promote the growth of the individual. By encouraging our employees to reach out and achieve their full potential, we enable them to make valuable contributions to ESI—while achieving their personal and professional goals. We will provide opportunities for individual achievement.

One of our key beliefs is that the nature of an organization is such that the results of team efforts quite often exceed those of individual effort. The power of a team decision is the mutual commitment to success that is built during the decision-making process. We place a high value on group achievement. We believe our people are fully capable of self-management. Further, we believe that if our objectives are clear and understood, the shared vision that results will enable our employees to manage themselves. The primary goal of management is to enable our people to succeed.

Stable employment and long-term commitment contribute to our company's success. We will strive to stabilize employment by staffing conservatively and utilize alternate resources to meet unusual business demands. We believe in sharing in the success of the organization. We also believe people seek their own rewards and that self-motivation is the best form of lasting motivation•

OUR SHAREHOLDERS

We believe building value for our shareholders is best done over time. That means we will manage the company for long-term earnings.

We are committed to earn an attractive return for our shareholders. We believe the best way to do that is to successfully meet our customer's needs. The result, if we do that well, will be the strong appreciation of shareholder investment, fostering a healthy partnership with our shareholders•

OUR SUPPLIERS

Building mutually beneficial partnerships with our key suppliers is important to our success. To accomplish this relationship, we will share our needs and requirements and endeavor to select suppliers who are willing to work in partnership with us•

PROFITABILITY

ESI's goal is to effectively provide high value products. By achieving that goal, we will earn superior returns on our resources which can be shared among our stakeholders.

Achieving superior results is essential to attract the resources we need to be successful. A long-term commitment to superior profitability is an essential condition for our growth and development as an organization•

IMPROVEMENT

ESI can never be satisfied with its performance. We must strive for continual improvement in all areas.

The productive and innovative use of our resources is critical to our long-term success. We will encourage prudent risk-taking, we will develop new and better products, we will devise more effective operating methods and we will organize our people to support a culture dedicated to MAKING THINGS HAPPEN.

As ESI grows, we must take advantage of our ever-increasing experience. A combination of excitement and aggressiveness is necessary if we are to remain the trendsetter—breaking new ground before others have perceived that a new opportunity exists•

SUCCESS

To remain static in an expanding field is to fall behind. But, growth for growth's sake is not our goal—nor do we believe rapid growth itself is a reliable measure of success. Success is the natural outcome of setting and achieving well-defined objectives through healthy, orderly growth. Success has many aspects: sales, profits, assets, technology, quality, job challenge, individual earnings, new products and services, and increasing personal knowledge and confidence. No one of these must be allowed to eclipse the others; a proper balance must be maintained•

COMMUNITY RESPONSIBILITY

As an international company, ESI has a responsibility to interact and respond to economic, political, social and cultural needs in communities where we do business.

We can best fulfill these responsibilities by providing high value products to our customers and rewarding careers for our people. Doing this successfully will enable ESI to take a leadership role in local communities, participate in resolving social problems, actively promote education and encourage involvement of ESI's people in the community•

SUMMER 1986

Exhibit 20. Electro Scientific Industries' Statement of Purpose

---

When reading a mission statement one caution should be observed: while it might seem logical that the higher priority items would be listed first and lower priority items last, such is not necessarily the case. All of the elements of the mission statement are important. Because of the interrelation of all of the elements, each is important in providing the foundation for the company's philosophy.

It is a highly competitive society in which we live. In fact, it is that competition which is the basis of our economic system. Because of the competition there are opportunities. Opportunities to compete for the customer's dollar and opportunities to achieve the "American Dream." Our economic system may not be perfect, but it has achieved a phenomenal record in slightly over two hundred years. While it is true that some factors are more important than others, forgetting any one of these critical elements can leave a company vulnerable to the competitive forces that drive our economic system.

The elements that make up a mission statement are basic traits. Individually, they represent basic elements of good business practice, but collectively they represent more.

Collectively the elements of a mission statement provide insight into the management style of the company. They spell out the company's goals and show where the priorities of a company lie. Together, the elements put forth in a company's mission statement help to define the company's personality. In the following chapters we shall examine each of the above traits in more detail.

6

The Most Important
Asset

Each company ranks its priorities in its own unique order. Yet time and
time again it's the employee who is considered to be the most valuable
asset of the company. It is the employee that makes it possible for the
company to be in business.

Recognition of the value of good employees is shown throughout many
mission statements. They bespeak high praise and point out the value of
the employee. Some of the more powerful statements are quoted below:

> "The employees of Styrotech Corporation are our greatest asset."
> (Styrotech Corporation's "Our Business Philosophy")

> "Our people are the source of our strength. They provide our
> corporate intelligence and determine our reputation and vitality.
> Involvement and teamwork are our core human values." (Ford
> Motor Company's "Company Mission, Values, and Guiding Prin-
> ciples")

> "To recognize the one limitless resource: the individual and col-
> lective potential of the human being." (Tektronix's "Statement of
> Corporate Intent")

> "People are key to Honeywell's success." ("Honeywell Princi-
> ples")

> "We believe that the most important asset of Westinghouse is its
> people—in every plant, office and community, wherever they work
> and live." ("Westinghouse Creed")

> "ESI's greatest resource is the individual and collective potential
> of our people." (Electro Scientific Industries' "Corporate State-
> ment of Purpose")

"We are dedicated to the belief that people are our most important asset." ("Worthington Industries' Philosophy")

"People are the key to StorageTek's success." (StorageTek's "Operating Principles")

"Dana people are our most important asset." (Dana Corporation's "Ten Key Thoughts")

"We believe that our basic objective can best be served by careful regard for our people; they determine our performance as a company." (Varian Associates' "Basic Corporate Objectives")

Perhaps it is not surprising that employees are considered a cherished asset in many of these companies. For some the largest expenditures incurred are for their employees. The costs include things such as salaries, benefits, retirement packages, and so on. When cost containment measures are necessary, it is rare for any company to reduce any of these expenditures.

Finding and keeping good employees are two very difficult tasks, but they are very important ones. The cost of keeping a good work force is very high. However, the cost of replacing a good work force is even higher. It would be impossible for any company to avoid turnover altogether, but keeping turnover within manageable proportions is crucial.

In the attempt to attract and keep employees, one thing is clear, it is in the best interest of both the employee and the company to keep the employees happy. All things considered, if an employee is happier with a job than he or she would be without it, he or she is likely to stay. On the other hand, if the employee would be happier without the job, he or she is likely to leave.

Although it would be impossible to have complete employee satisfaction, a great deal of effort goes into setting up an environment in which the employees will be content. One example of a company that goes to great lengths to keep its employees is the Federated Department Stores. Its commitment to its employees is spelled out in its "Priority on People." In this document, Federated sets this goal to "be—and be recognized as—the industry leader, the best, number one, the place to be, because of its people and the enlightened manner in which they are utilized."

Part of attracting and keeping good employees is matching the right person to the right job. Making this match is difficult yet important. Tektronix addresses this problem in its "Statement of Corporate Intent." They explain it in this way, " 'The right person for the right job' means we have to keep at two seemingly opposed tasks: One is to grow people, helping the individual expand to meet the next day's challenges—and, through effective grouping, attain larger and longer-term goals. The other is to increase the challenges themselves, so the job we offer will extend or even

CSX CORPORATION

MANAGEMENT STATEMENT

The success of CSX Corporation in meeting both the challenges of today and the opportunities of the future depends upon employees performing their jobs to the maximum of their abilities. Our objective is to provide a work environment which supports that high level of job performance and encourages employees to qualify themselves for greater responsibilities in the future. We believe this objective is best accomplished when employees work in an environment characterized by the following:

- *Management understands that employees respond positively both to responsibility and to freedom to participate, and that increased employee satisfaction will result in improved productivity, providing the company with a competitive edge;*

- *As a consequence, decision-making is delegated to the lowest possible level and employees are encouraged to become involved in the operation of the company, where their ideas are sought and acted upon;*

- *Employees understand the company's overall plans and objectives, as well as the goals of their departments, and they realize the importance of their personal contribution to the achievement of these goals;*

- *All employees, regardless of age, sex, race or any other potentially discriminating factor, are treated fairly and considerately and a spirit of trust and support exists between them and their supervisors;*

- *There is an awareness that two of management's most important responsibilities are to constructively evaluate employee performance, and to encourage employee professional growth and development.*

- *To that end, systems of reward and recognition exist throughout the company which recognize outstanding performance and encourage each employee's best efforts in the future. The achievement of such a work environment requires the personal leadership of senior management and the dedicated effort of all managers throughout the company.*

Exhibit 21. CSX Corporation's "Management Statement"

GENERAL SIGNAL can achieve its objectives only through the combined efforts of each person at all levels in the organization working together toward common objectives. The objectives should be realistic, should be clearly understood, and should reflect General Signal's basic character and personality.

It is management's responsibility to establish the objectives and to provide the best possible climate for their attainment.

Our Specific OBJECTIVES are these:

I.   To serve as good custodians of our stockholders' invested capital by enhancing its value through consistent growth in profits and return on investment.

II.   To let our growth be limited only by our ability to develop and produce equipment and systems of high value that satisfy real customer needs.

III.   To provide our employees with competitive salaries and wages, opportunity for personal growth, and a working environment that enables each to feel needed and wanted.

The CLIMATE should be characterized by:

I.   A commitment to excellence in every aspect of our business.

II.   A good feeling about the company at all employee levels—a feeling of mutual trust and mutual caring.

III.   Enthusiasm at all levels. Each person in a management position should be enthusiastic in ways that will engender enthusiasm throughout the organization.

IV.   A determination to be and be recognized as the leader, the #1 company—as to technology, product quality and service—in each of the markets we serve.

V.   High standards of business conduct and civic responsibility.

Exhibit 22. General Signal, Credo

HONEYWELL PRINCIPLES

Honeywell is an international corporation
whose goal is to work together with customers to
develop and apply advanced technologies through products,
systems and services, which in turn serve primarily to improve productivity,
conserve resources and meet aerospace and defense needs.
Honeywell adheres to the following principles.

Profits - Profitable operations are necessary to assure the continued health and growth of the company. Honeywell expects profits which equal or exceed those of leading international companies.

Integrity - Honeywell believes in the highest level of integrity and ethical behavior in relationships with customers, employees, shareholders, vendors, neighbors and governments.

Customers - Honeywell is dedicated to serving customers through excellence of product, systems and service, and through working together with customers to find the answers to their problems.

People - People are key to Honeywell's success. The company actively and affirmatively attracts and promotes the best people without regard to age, race, sex, creed, disability or nationality, and rewards them on their performance. Honeywell provides an environment for open, timely communications, safe working conditions, and opportunities for personal growth and accomplishment. Honeywell respects the dignity and privacy of individuals and believes in a climate of trust, cooperation and employee involvement.

Quality - Quality of product, application and service is essential to continue Honeywell's success. Quality improvement should pervade every job within the company. Honeywell believes quality results from an environment in which people work together to sustain excellence.

Decision-making - Honeywell believes sound growth is necessary to successful company performance. This is achieved through well-managed risk taking, innovation and entrepreneurship. Honeywell is committed to a decentralized structure in which business decisions are made at the lowest appropriate level.

Citizenship - Honeywell operates in compliance with all applicable laws and in ways that build a lasting reputation for integrity and good citizenship in all countries where it does business. The company encourages employees to become involved in community and national affairs. Honeywell manages its business in ways that are sensitive to the environment and that conserve natural resources.

Chairman and Chief Executive Officer

Exhibit 23. "Honeywell Principles"

surpass existing skills. Allowing a person to remain bigger than the job invites boredom; allowing the job to remain bigger than the person invites frustration."

Once the match is made by having the right person in the right job, the job does not end there. There are several other things that help the company maintain a stable work force. An important element in obtaining a stable work force is to achieve a high level of employee morale. Again, an employee is likely to stay with a company if that is his or her best alternative. Because the employee's morale is an important key to job satisfaction, many companies go to great lengths to achieve this goal.

Texaco is one company that outlines its formula for building morale. In its "Guiding Principles and Objectives," Texaco sets this objective: "To maintain a high level of employee morale through fostering by example an atmosphere of hard work, recognize dignity of the individual by treating every person in the Company with respect and courtesy, provide opportunities for employees to develop and advance to the utmost of their capabilities, encourage and carefully consider all suggestions from employees and if not acceptable explain reasons why to the employee, pay compensation which compares favorably with others in the industry, and provide safe and efficient places in which to work."

As can be seen from the above passage, obtaining a high level of employee morale is difficult and requires many tasks to be accomplished simultaneously. Like Texaco, many companies specify their formula for achieving high morale in their mission statements. Some are less specific, while others are more so.

Foundations for an Uncommon Company

OUR RELATIONSHIPS:

We should treat others as we would be treated . . . with dignity, respect, integrity and honesty. This applies to:

- Associates & their families
- Customers
  Consumers
  Health Care Providers
  Wholesalers
- Stockholders

- Suppliers
- Financial Community & General Public

Those who produce should share in the results. Each Marion associate has the right to:

- Be treated as an individual
- Be rewarded for performance
- Know what is expected on the job and where we stand in relation to that expectation.
- Get problems resolved and be heard
- A safe and healthy workplace
- Share in the growth of the company through personal & career growth

We earn these through our high productivity and commitment to quality in all that we do.

OUR RESPONSIBILITIES:

1. We have a responsibility to our shareholders to build the business on their behalf. This requires prudent investment in the development of the people, products, and facilities necessary to sustain long-term growth in profits and return on shareholder investment.

2. We have a special responsibility to our associates, our customers, and to society to provide products and service of the highest quality and to conduct our business with integrity and the highest ethical standards.

3. Risk taking is an inherent factor in business, and we are prepared to manage high risk relative to our markets—but any risk should be taken by the corporation itself and never at the expense of the consumer, the customer, or any Marion associate.

4. We have a responsibility for excellence and innovation...We do all that we do to the very best of our ability and with the strongest enthusiasm we can generate. It is the very nature of our business to do things that have never been done before and for which there are always reasons they cannot be done. Success for us requires the ability and the spirit to find a pathway through any obstacle, even when no pathway is visible at the start.

Exhibit 24. Marion Laboratories' "Foundations for an Uncommon Company"

High morale among the employees can be accomplished by paying attention to specific basic elements of good morale. Some of these specifics include recognizing the dignity of the individual, allowing the employee to grow within the organization, fostering a spirit of teamwork, and so on.

The first of these elements, recognizing the dignity of the individual, is quite simply stated in the "Westinghouse Creed," which states, "We believe in the dignity of every employee in Westinghouse and the importance of his work."

Another company that addresses this concern for its employees is the Hughes Tool Company. In their "Corporate Philosophy" they state, "The Hughes Tool Company believes that all human beings have a basic dignity, and we will build on their talents and strengths. It is a thrilling experience to develop PEOPLE, PRODUCTS, and PROSPERITY."

In their mission statements many companies have shown that a second important aspect in obtaining a high level of employee morale is allowing the employees to grow within the company. People often have a need to feel important. They like to have a sense of self worth. Part of this can be obtained by growing as an individual, by taking on more responsibility, and by contributing more.

A company can help good employees become better by allowing them to grow within the corporation. It is in the best interest of both the company and the employee to provide the opportunities for personal growth. Electro Scientific Industries (ESI) recognizes and addresses this concept in their mission statement. In their "Corporate Statement of Purpose," ESI states, "We believe one of our critical responsibilities is to promote the growth of the individual. By encouraging our employees to reach out and achieve their full potential, we enable them to make valuable contributions to ESI—while achieving their personal and professional goals. We will provide opportunities for individual achievement."

Another element that is often helpful in obtaining high morale involves getting all employees to work together as a team. By promoting the teamwork concept, both the company and the employees realize a greater worth. Regardless of how good employees are, they seldom work alone. To be of maximum value to a company, they must be able to work well together.

Some companies stress the teamwork concept in their mission statements. Two such companies are the Ford Motor Company and Baxter Travenol Laboratories. In its mission statement Ford states, "Employee involvement is our way of life—We are a team. We must treat each other with trust and respect." In a similar sentiment, Baxter Travenol sets this objective in its mission to "promote an environment for employees that fosters teamwork, personal growth and respect for the individual."

A secondary benefit companies derive from promoting teamwork is that teamwork helps the company achieve the two previously mentioned objectives: recognizing the dignity of the individual and allowing the individual to grow. Companies recognize that by working together as a team, people can generally achieve more than working alone. Since there is often a greater sense of accomplishment working with a team, the person's self esteem is enhanced.

A fourth element important to developing high morale is to provide stable employment for the employee. Most people depend on their job to provide a means of living. The paycheck is certainly not the only reward, but it is an essential one. Even those employees who do not need the money would find it difficult to stay if the paychecks stopped altogether.

Like the other traits discussed, the stability of employment is addressed in the mission statements of some companies. An example of this can be found in ESI's "Corporate Statement of Purpose": "Stable employment and long-term commitment contribute to our company's success. We will strive to stabilize employment by staffing conservatively and utilize alternate resources to meet unusual business demands."

A final element often stressed is a company's commitment to equal opportunity. This sentiment is found in many mission statements; some examples follow: "There must be equal opportunity for employment, development and advancement for those qualified" (Johnson & Johnson's "Our Credo"); "The company actively and affirmatively attracts and promotes the best people without regard to age, race, sex, creed, disability or nationality, and rewards them on their performance" ("Honeywell Principles"); and "To create an environment in which, without discrimination, all employees are enabled, encouraged and stimulated to perform at their highest potential of output and creativity and to attain the greatest possible level of job satisfaction in the spirit of the Westinghouse Creed" ("The Westinghouse Purpose").

So far we have been concentrating on the commitments of a company to its employees. We have stressed how both the company and their employees benefit from living up to these responsibilities. In reality, however, this is a two way street. Clearly, employees have reciprocal responsibilities to their employers.

Although few companies state what they expect in return from their employees, some do. These things are generally items most people would naturally expect from a loyal workforce.

It is interesting to note that most companies set some very difficult goals for themselves, while expecting much less from employees. Those companies that do specify what is expected from employees require only basic traits from them.

"From employees we expect an honest day's work for an honest day's pay." ("Worthington Industries' Philosophy")

"We expect our management to operate with genuine interest in the welfare, security, and aspirations of our employees. We desire

PRIORITY ON PEOPLE

How Human Resources Are To Be Managed In Federated

INTRODUCTION

While such factors as market position, retailing format, control of critical resources, and national policy cannot be dismissed, for the most part the achievements of Federated and its divisions are the direct result of the combined efforts of each individual in the company. In the final analysis, it is our people who make the difference. This is true of the past, and current management's ability to attract, hire, mobilize, keep, challenge, and grow valuable, talented people will determine the success of the corporation in the future. Consequently, no higher priority exists for Federated and its divisions than to be--and be recognized as--the industry leader, the best, number one, the place to be, because of its people and the enlightened manner in which they are utilized.

GUIDING PRINCIPLES

To achieve and sustain this unique position, Federated and its divisions are expected to:

1. Employ the most effective and productive people in the retail industry. Also create work environments that serve to retain these people and allow them to enjoy their work without sacrificing organizational commitments in the process.

2. Consider dignity and respect for the individual as the most important human consideration influencing our daily decisions.

3. Live by the highest standards of executive conduct. We intend for our decisions and actions to be consistently beyond question from an ethical standpoint.

4. Provide ample growth opportunities for our associates. While we expect the individual to take responsibility for his/her own development, every manager is also expected to, consistent with corporate objectives, plan the necessary time and effort required to guide the development of his/her subordinates. Wherever possible, we will attempt to make individual work assignments consistent with personal career objectives.

5. Operate with an open and above-board management style. We will insist that problems and decisions be openly discussed, and allowed to be challenged without retribution, and people be fully informed and involved as an integral part of the way to manage the organization. Once decisions are final, however, we will expect everyone to support these decisions, and work as a team to effectively implement them.

6. Embrace the idea that individual initiative is a highly prized virtue. If something needs to be done, we want each and every employee to feel they personally have the freedom, obligation and responsibility to see that it gets done, and done right. It is our intent to see that those who effectively apply this concept are amply rewarded.

RESULTING BUSINESS ENVIRONMENT

The consistent application of these guiding principles over time is expected to lead to a business environment that is marked by the following characteristics:

1. Strategies and objectives are jointly constructed, widely shared and constantly discussed. There is significant commitment and a strong, consistent flow of effort toward the achievement of those objectives.

2. People freely point out the existence of problems because they expect them to be dealt with fairly and are optimistic that they can be solved.

3. Problem solving is highly pragmatic. In attacking problems, people work informally and are not preoccupied with status, territory or guessing what higher management will think.

4. Management faces up to difficult decisions, whether they are business, organizational or individual in nature.

5. Open (constructive) confrontation is viewed as important to decision making and personal growth. People say what they want, allow others to do the same, and never hit below the belt.

6. When there is a crisis, people at all levels band together, help each other, and work on it until the crisis is over.

7. There is a great deal of on-the-job learning based on a willingness to give, seek, and use feedback and advice. Feedback on performance is routine and helpful. People see themselves as capable of significant personal development and growth.

8. People are "turned on" and highly involved by choice. They are optimistic and view the workplace as important and fun.

9. Relationships are supportive and honest (not characterized by an underlying fear or mistrust). People generally know what is important to the organization and what is not. There is a high degree of trust throughout the organization.

10. Risk is accepted as a condition of growth and change. "What can we learn from each mistake?" is management's view of things.

11. Recognition and rewards are considered important to people. Compensation is dealt with honestly and consistently based on level of contribution and responsibility, both in the short and long term.

BOTTOM LINE IMPACT

The ultimate measure of our success in satisfying this priority on people will be the resultant financial performance of Federated and its divisions, and the market to book price ratio of Federated stock versus that of other retailers against which we measure ourselves over time.

Exhibit 25. Federated Department Stores' "Priority on People"

ⓦ Westinghouse Creed

We believe that the most important asset of Westinghouse is its people – in every plant, office and community, wherever they work and live.

We believe in the dignity of every employe in Westinghouse and the importance of his work.

We believe that the well-being and security of employes are dependent upon the soundness and security of Westinghouse; that, to keep our Company sound and secure, the people of Westinghouse have an obligation to make the most effective use of their skill, effort and time on their jobs.

We believe that all of the people of Westinghouse must recognize our joint responsibility to the owners of our Company, to the public we serve and to our nation as a whole.

In recognition of these beliefs, and of the Company's responsibilities to employes, we pledge:

To treat every employe fairly, with consideration and respect, expecting all who supervise the work of others to treat those under their direction as they themselves would want to be treated.

To pay wages and provide employe benefits that fairly reward employes for their skill, effort and time.

To weigh all decisions with full regard for their effect on the well-being of employes.

To try to provide stability of employment to the greatest practical extent.

To listen to and handle with fairness and promptness the complaint of any employe.

To provide employes every possible opportunity for self-improvement and advancement in the Company.

To provide good working conditions – a safe, clean friendly workplace and proper facilities to help the employe do his job effectively.

Exhibit 26. "Westinghouse Creed"

that all employees develop a similar interest in the company, knowing and sharing its goals." (Varian Associates, "Basic Corporate Objectives")

"All employees are expected to be 100% honest." (Hughes Tool Company's "Corporate Philosophy")

It seems logical that when a company and its employees are working together to achieve common goals, their association will be mutually beneficial. On the other hand, when they are at odds with each other, the potential for difficult times is readily apparent.

Although it would be impossible to develop a magic formula for perfecting this relationship between the employee and the employer, many companies work toward this goal. They have recognized the need and believe in its importance.

It is difficult to prioritize and express a corporation's responsibilities in a brief document such as a mission statement. It is even more difficult when trying to describe something that is the foundation on which the company is built. Since companies are often the result of the actions of their employees, the task of briefly describing the commitment to employees is extremely difficult.

Despite the difficulty, most companies accept the challenge. They attempt to describe their commitments to their employees in their mission statements. In summarizing this chapter, let's look at how some companies express their concerns for their employees:

"We are responsible to our employees, the men and women who work with us throughout the world. Everyone must be considered as an individual. We must respect their dignity and recognize their merit. They must have a sense of security in their jobs. Compensation must be fair and adequate, and working conditions safe. Employees must feel free to make suggestions and complaints. There must be equal opportunity for employment, development and advancement for those qualified. We must provide competent management, and their actions must be just and ethical." (Johnson & Johnson's "Our Credo")

"The company actively and affirmatively attracts and promotes the best people without regard to age, race, sex, creed, disability or nationality, and rewards them on their performance. Honeywell provides an environment for open, timely communications, safe working conditions, and opportunities for personal growth and accomplishment. Honeywell respects the dignity and privacy

HUGHES TOOL COMPANY

Corporate Objectives and Philosophy

THE HUGHES TOOL COMPANY IS COMMITTED TO GROWTH THROUGH SERVICE TO THE INDUSTRIES IN WHICH IT IS, OR MAY BECOME INVOLVED.

TO GROW AND EXPAND THE HUGHES TOOL COMPANY MUST MANUFACTURE AND DISTRIBUTE HIGH QUALITY PRODUCTS, AND PROVIDE COMPETENT CUSTOMER AND IN-COMPANY SERVICES, AND THEREBY ACHIEVE AN ADEQUATE RETURN ON CAPITAL EMPLOYED—RECOGNIZING THAT PROFITS ARE THE KEYSTONE OF A BUSINESS STRUCTURE WHICH MAKE POSSIBLE THE ATTAINMENT OF ALL OTHER OBJECTIVES, SUCH AS:

> TO FULFILL OUR RESPONSIBILITY TO OUR CUSTOMERS BY PROVIDING PRODUCTS OF HIGH QUALITY INCORPORATING THE ADVANCES OF OUR TECHNOLOGICAL RESEARCH AND EXPERIENCE, BY PROVIDING COMPETENT SALES AND SERVICE, AND BY SEEKING TO OFFER THE GREATEST VALUE BY KEEPING OUR COSTS LOW.

> TO FULFILL OUR RESPONSIBILITY TO THE COMMUNITIES IN WHICH WE OPERATE BY PROVIDING FAIR AND JUST EMPLOYMENT OPPORTUNITIES, PARTICIPATING IN WORTHWHILE CIVIC ACTIVITIES, AND PAYING OUR FAIR SHARE OF TAXES.

> TO FULFILL OUR RESPONSIBILITY TO THOSE WHO WORK WITH US BY PAYING FAIR AND ADEQUATE WAGES, PROVIDING CLEAN AND SAFE WORKING CONDITIONS, OFFERING EQUAL OPPORTUNITIES FOR INDIVIDUAL DEVELOPMENT AND ADVANCEMENT, AND PROVIDING MAXIMUM JOB SECURITY.

> TO FULFILL OUR RESPONSIBILITY TO OUR STOCKHOLDERS WHO EXPECT THE COMPANY TO GROW AND PRODUCE AN ADEQUATE RETURN ON INVESTMENT.

HUGHES TOOL COMPANY

CORPORATE PHILOSOPHY

The Hughes Tool Company believes that all human beings have a basic dignity, and we will build on their talents and strengths. It is a thrilling experience to develop PEOPLE, PRODUCTS, and PROSPERITY.

We believe that all work is dignified, to get the most from life, one must WORK HARD and toward realistic OBJECTIVES.

Employees will be counseled and coached on the basis of *planned* objectives versus objectives *reached*. Busyness and activity alone will not replace actual accomplishments with regard to formulated OBJECTIVES.

We believe in the continuation of a free-enterprise system in this country, and hopefully, in the world where people must produce in order to participate in the rewards. We further believe in freedom of political, social and spiritual systems.

All employees are expected to be 100-percent honest. We believe all laws of the lands should be obeyed. If we disagree with the law, work hard within the law to have it changed.

Everyone has more potential than they think. A self-confident person will receive more rewards than others. People must know themselves to be really successful. They must have courage to SELL THEIR STRENGTHS or they will accept and be handicapped by their weaknesses. Utilization of STRENGTHS will usually correct the weaknesses.

Looking out for one's own interest is natural and normal, but personal interest can be fully realized only through and by development of others. Happiness comes by giving knowledge, words of encouragement, guidance, constructive criticism, words of faith, and material things.

People are likely to be happier when they have deep personal RELIGIOUS FAITH.

The ONLY REASON for our JOBS and FINANCIAL REWARD is to help our company to realize its OBJECTIVE to produce a FAIR RETURN ON INVESTMENT and GROW by reinvestment. Profit is good and not bad. Each employee should completely understand and be convinced of this fact.

Exhibit 27. "Hughes Tool Company Corporate Objectives and Philosophy"

of individuals and believes in a climate of trust, cooperation and employee involvement." ("Honeywell Principles")

"To maintain a highly productive, energetic, and loyal organization of men and women by selecting and training capable employees and by providing good working conditions, competent leadership, compensation on the basis of performance, opportunity for growth and development, and a high degree of employment security." (Armstrong's "Objectives")

7

The Measure of Success

A second element that has a very high priority in the mission statements of most companies is the profit objective. Almost all of the companies that have mission statements specify their profit motive there. Some are specific, while others are more general. Before looking at specific references to profit in various mission statements, let's look at what "profit" truly means.

Basically, profit represents the difference between the cost of producing a product or service, and the value of that product or service. A company that fails to produce a profit utilizes more resources than it produces. On the other hand, a company that produces a profit is providing more value from the resources it uses.

Profit then can be thought of as a tool for measuring economic performance. It measures how well a company is operating within our economic system. The Ford Motor Company defines profit in this way. In their "Company Mission, Values, and Guiding Principles," they state, "Profits are the ultimate measure of how efficiently we provide customers with the best products for their needs."

There are certainly exceptions to the above rules, such as monopolies, nonprofit organizations, and governments. In a purely free enterprise system, however, these generalizations hold true. The profit motive is a force that drives our economic system. While other economic systems do not rely so heavily on the profit motive, the free enterprise system does.

Realizing the value of profit is the key. There are some people who have come to believe that profit is somehow evil. They think that some large corporations are making profits that are simply too big. Yet realizing what profits represent, they can best be viewed as a reward for a job well done.

One company that points to the value of profit in its mission statement is the Hughes Tool Company. In its "Corporate Objectives and Philosophy," Hughes states, "Profit is good and not bad. Each employee should be completely convinced of this fact."

Having explained profit, it is also important to realize that it is successful attainment of the profit objective that make the other objectives possible. This idea is also expressed in the "Corporate Philosophy" of the Hughes Tool Company: "Profits are the keystone of a business structure which make possible the attainment of all other objectives."

Beyond the philosophical definitions, the importance of profit can be described simply. In its mission statement, the Ford Motor Company de-

---

The Westinghouse Purpose

The basic purpose of Westinghouse, in all its decisions and actions, is:

1) To attain a continuous high level of profit which places it in the top ranks of industry in its rate of return on invested capital, recognizing that Westinghouse can serve society only if it is financially viable.

2) To operate all elements of the Corporation throughout the world in a manner which contributes to the improvement of society and which is sensitive to the natural and human environment.

3) To achieve steady growth in profits, sales volume and highly productive investment at rates exceeding those of the national economy as a whole.

4) To be responsive at all times to the needs of customers and of people by providing quality products and services, by improving them continuously and by creating new products and services which increase user satisfaction.

5) To distribute equitably among owners, employes and customers the fruits of improved productivity and efficient use of management, labor and capital.

6) To maintain a dynamic business structure by continuously shifting investment from areas which have lost their profit vitality into new business fields where potential for growth is high.

7) To create an environment in which, without discrimination, all employes are enabled, encouraged and stimulated to perform at their highest potential of output and creativity and to attain the greatest possible level of job satisfaction in the spirit of the Westinghouse Creed.

8) To conduct all affairs of the Corporation in conformance with the highest ethical and legal standards.

These eight points are indivisible. Together, as a unit, they express the basic purpose and fundamental management philosophy of the Westinghouse Electric Corporation.

Exhibit 28. "The Westinghouse Purpose"

scribes the importance of profits in this way, "Profits are required to survive and grow."

While profit is not the only objective of a successful company, it is a crucial one. There are many other objectives to be achieved. Each company determines for itself how these objectives must be balanced to meet its individual needs.

The Sun Company, in "The Creed We Work By," puts its profit goals in perspective by stating, "We believe that while business cannot survive if incapable of performing profitably, its sole obligation does not consist literally of producing profits."

By surveying the treatment of profit in mission statements, we can see two things that profit does for a company. First, it generates money so the owners of the company can be repaid for their investment, and second, it provides economic support that allows the company to grow.

The first of these is repaying the stockholders. Many companies feel that this is not only a goal, but an obligation. A corporation, whether privately or publicly held, is owned by its stockholders. The stockholders have invested their money in good faith and they have the right to hope to realize a profit from their investment.

Corporations have the obligation to protect the stockholder's investment. In its "Corporate Objectives," the Hughes Tool Company supports this responsibility when it sets this as one of its objectives: "To fulfill our

---

Statement of Business Mission
Metropolitan Life Insurance Company

Metropolitan's business mission is to help meet the financial security needs of our existing and potential customers. We will continue to meet the traditional income protection/continuation and savings needs of individuals (directly and through group plans) and the financing needs of the public and private sectors. We will also seek opportunities to use our resources to serve more fully the broader financial security needs of our customers and the marketplace. To meet this mission, we will consider acquisitions as well as other modes of business diversification.

The foundation for our future growth and source of competitive advantage will be the size and scope of our existing customer base, the economic advantages derived from our broad-based operations, our financial strength, and our reputation for integrity and fair dealing. We will seek to use these strengths effectively and to build on them in serving our current customers and in seeking to expand the range of our business activities.

In establishing strategies for each of our core businesses, as well as in evaluating new opportunities to expand our basic business focus, we will seek to:

1. Participate fully in the growth of our traditional businesses by establishing a position in major geographic and demographic segments.

2. Develop or acquire capabilities necessary to meet more fully the evolving financial security and related needs of our core business customers, including positions in new or emerging financial security markets.

3. Build a position in each of our core businesses that offers Metropolitan an opportunity to exercise market leadership.

4. Earn an adequate rate of return from the resources employed in each of our businesses—both capital and manpower—to ensure a sound financial base.

In establishing objectives for each of our businesses, we will measure our performance on the basis of our impact on the areas in which we operate rather than simply the size of our operations. We will seek to maintain an above average rate of growth in each business, allowing us to meet the ongoing needs of our customers, maintain a position of market leadership, and attract and retain the quality individuals we need to achieve our objectives. We will also seek a rate of return from each business that will protect our financial position and provide the growth in our capital base necessary to meet our obligations to current and future customers.

Exhibit 29. Metropolitan Life Insurance Company's "Statement of Business Mission"

---

responsibility to our stockholders who expect the company to grow and produce an adequate return on investment."

In a similar statement, Electro Scientific Industries states, "Our responsibility to the owners of the company is a long-term obligation to provide return on their investment."

The Dana Corporation goes one step beyond this by stating, in its "Policies," "The purpose of the Dana Corporation is to earn money for its shareholders and to increase the value of their investment. We believe the best way to do this is to earn an acceptable return by properly utilizing our assets and controlling our cash."

For some companies, profit is the first priority. For others, it takes on secondary importance. And still others consider profit last.

Among those that list profits as their primary objective is Worthington Industries. They state in their "Philosophy," "The first corporate goal for Worthington Industries is to earn money for its shareholders and increase the value of their investment."

Another company placing profits at the top of its priorities is the Dow Chemical Company. The first of their "Objectives" is "To seek maximum long-term profit growth as the primary means to ensure the prosperity and well-being of our employees, stockholders and our customers by making products that the people of the world need, and to do so better than anyone else."

Although profit is certainly a high priority in all companies, a few mention profits last in their mission statements. This may, at first glance, appear to be a little contradictory, but it can be explained easily by looking at an example of one company that places profits last.

Among those which place profits as the last of their objectives is Johnson & Johnson. In "Our Credo," it states, "Our final responsibility is to our stockholders. Business must make a sound profit."

Although putting profits last may seem unwise, Johnson & Johnson feels that by following the other principles of the Credo, profit will naturally follow. This too is summed up in the final sentence of the Credo, "When we operate according to these principles, the stockholders should realize a fair return."

A second result of producing a profit is to generate the capital that allows the company to grow. The money required to support corporate activities at all levels comes from the profits produced. At Armstrong this idea is expressed in its "Objectives": "To earn sufficient profit on the capital employed in the enterprise to provide for continuing growth."

Texaco's statement ties several profit objectives together by setting the objective "to be financially sound and responsible, pay fair return to the shareholders for the use of their capital, maintain a record of productivity and profits which will enable the Company to attract new capital and continue to grow and expand its earning power, and through inspired leadership and effective teamwork strive to be the most highly respected company in the industry."

Another important aspect of the profit motive is that it provides the thrust to stimulate production. Perhaps one of the strongest statements to this effect can be found in Sun Company's "The Creed We Work By," where it states, "We believe economic competition spurred by the profit motive gives unparalleled thrust to production, provides the material base for superior living standards, and preserves the widest latitude for the exercise of individual preferences."

While some companies aim to produce a "sufficient" profit, others want

Ferro Corporation
Broad Statement of Mission

Recognizing its obligation to its shareholders, Ferro will be organized and managed in a manner to achieve steady growth in earnings, enhancement of shareholder equity, and dividend payout commensurate with earnings growth.

Management efforts will be focused on attaining the optimum combination of profit growth, return on investment, and financial stability compatible with the Corporation's resources. These efforts will be consistent with its responsibilities to shareholders, customers, employees, governments and the general public.

The broad objective is to achieve superior performance according to these criteria:

- Rate of return on shareholder equity.
- Growth in earnings.

Over the long term, the level of profitability will provide the funds necessary to support the Company's business growth. Additional sources of profit may be funded through the prudent employment of cash, debt, and/or stock.

The Company's operations will be directed to meeting the needs of customers through the development and marketing of specialty materials, engineered products and services worldwide. These businesses will have sufficient size, technical scope and market position to provide opportunities for current and future growth.

Our reputation is one of our most valued assets. We will conduct our business on sound ethical principles based on integrity and fairness to all our constituencies.

While our ultimate responsibility is to our shareholders, we have a deep commitment to our employees whose skills, attitudes, and efforts are essential to the success of the Company. Achievement of sustained growth and profitability objectives will provide our employees the opportunities for personal career advancement and commensurate rewards. We will maintain a work environment which will enable our employees to develop and contribute to their maximum potential.

Exhibit 30. Ferro Corporation's "Broad Statement of Mission"

Corporate Objectives
SLRP 1983

As one of the most important forces in electronics, we at Intel have a mission: To drive the technological revolution by aggressively advancing technology and delivering its benefits to the world.

We will fulfill this mission through pursuit of the following series of objectives.

1. Use our technological leadership to achieve a pre-eminent position in the businesses we pursue.

    A. Grow as fast as the markets we serve.

    B. Maintain an average of at least 10% after-tax margin and, at all times, the highest margins of major companies in our industry.

    C. Concentrate on those areas of business where we can have a commanding position (either #1 or #2) and in which our combination of capabilities result in uniquely strong competitive advantages; to maintain a position in other business areas only if it is important to develop or support the commanding positions.

    D. To be and be recognized as a technology leader in those areas we pursue: To exploit our technologies fully for both new product development and the attainment of design-to-cost goals.

2. Operate our business in a manner which enhances the strong mutual commitment between Intel and its employees.

    A. Minimize the disruptive fluctuations caused by business cycles and capricious competitors so that our long term commitments to people and programs to which they are committed can be maintained.

    B. Seek out, attract and retain the best people possible at all levels and provide them with challenging jobs, training and opportunities for personal growth so that they may share in Intel's success.

3. Be a valued contributor to and supporter of our customers, vendors and the communities in which we operate.

    A. Be and be recognized as the leader in meeting our customers' needs for delivery, reliability, quality and service.

    B. Conduct our business with customers and vendors and in our internal activities with integrity and professionalism.

    C. Be an asset to the countries and communities in which we operate.

Exhibit 31. Intel Corporation's "Corporate Objectives"

more. Some companies feel it is important that its profits are maximized. This thought is most strongly held in those companies in the financial industry. Perhaps this is explained easily when you consider that profit is the product that is produced by companies in this industry.

Two companies which, in their mission statements, seek to maximize profits are Varian Associates, Inc. and the Chase Manhattan Bank. For Varian, the objective is simply stated: "Our primary objective is to produce for our shareholders the maximum return on their investment in the company."

At Chase the profit objective is somewhat more complex. In the "Chase Vision" we find, "We intend to be the best performer in the markets we

---

Chase Vision

CHASE

A VISION OF LEADERSHIP

As a broad-based, world-class financial institution, Chase will play a leadership role in the global financial marketplace. We intend to be the best performer in the markets we choose to serve, performing at a level second to none over a sustained period of time. We will be highly profitable, achieving a return on equity and assets at the highest level of the worldwide financial industry. We recognize the absolute requirement to maintain our financial strength. At the same time, we will continue to exemplify the highest standards of corporate responsibility and leadership in the communities we serve.

BEING THE BEST IN AN UNCERTAIN WORLD

A Volatile Environment. Our future challenge is significantly heightened by the nature of the environment we will be operating within for the rest of this century. Surely we will see accelerating international interdependence and continuing volatility. In addition, increased deregulation of world financial markets, particularly in the U.S., will result in our aggressively competing in a series of new markets, not only against our traditional competition, but also against an expanded universe of new competitors.

Capitalizing on Change. Though difficult, this environment will provide significant opportunities for institutions that can effectively manage change, respond to the need for technological innovation, and take advantage of market opportunities.

OUR STRENGTHS

As a result of our financial strength, size, broad geographic network, diversified customer base, highly professional staff, and broad product and service capability, our unique franchise positions us well to lead the competition in this challenging environment.

OUR GOALS

We will be the top performer in our chosen markets by providing productive and innovative financial services to corporations, institutions, and individuals. Corporations and institutions will be assisted in achieving sound, productive growth. Individuals will be provided with a broad range of products and services to meet their financial needs.

MANAGING TO BE THE BEST

Optimum performance demands that our organizational focus be market-driven. Therefore, we will structure ourselves to maximize our capacity to respond effectively to changing customer needs on a timely basis, and with the highest level of innovation. Responsibility and accountability will be driven downward throughout the organization, consistent with prudent management, so that our people will feel a deep sense of ownership for and commitment to the organization as a whole.

OUR CORE VALUES—TEAMWORK. EXCELLENCE. QUALITY. INTEGRITY. COMMITMENT.

To achieve the highest level of synergy, teamwork will underscore and drive our efforts, and be a core value in our culture.

We will set the highest performance standards for both individuals and business units; invest in our people and help them develop the knowledge and skills necessary to meet these standards; demand performance consistent with such standards; and reward our people in accordance with those standards.

We will achieve our goals through a dedication to quality, integrity, and excellence in everything we do. This will be clearly visible in the commitment and care we extend to our shareholders, our customers, and our people.

Exhibit 32. Chase Manhattan Bank's "Chase Vision"

Our Objectives

A company can perform effectively only when it strives to attain specified objectives through the application of definite principles. At United Parcel Service, our objectives and principles have not sprung forth suddenly. They represent the experience of dedicated and imaginative people, from our company's beginning to the present day.

OUR OBJECTIVES ARE:

To fulfill a useful economic purpose—satisfying the need for prompt, dependable delivery of small packages, serving all shippers and receivers wherever they may be located within our service areas—with the best possible service at the lowest possible cost to the public.

To maintain a strong, forward-looking, efficient, and cooperative organization which will be ever mindful of the well-being of our people and enable them to develop their individual capabilities.

To keep the ownership and control of our company in the hands of its managers and supervisors—to build an organization of people who think and act as partners rather than as "hired hands."

To maintain a financially strong company earning a reasonable profit—which is the only way we can provide security for the members of our organization, continue to provide quality service for our customers, and reward our share-owners with dividends and increases in value of the shares in which their money is invested.

To develop additional profitable businesses which complement our efforts to maintain a financially strong company.

To be alert to changing conditions and ready at all times to adjust our viewpoints and operations to meet them.

To earn and preserve a reputation as a company whose well-being is in the public interest and whose people are respected for their performance, character, and integrity.

To establish and maintain a high standard of excellence in everything we do.

Exhibit 33. United Parcel Service's "Our Objectives"

choose to serve, performing at a level second to none over a sustained period of time. We will be highly profitable, achieving a return on equity and assets at the highest level of the worldwide financial industry. We recognize the absolute requirement to maintain our financial strength."

Chase has set its goals high. It wants to be at the top of its field. Notice how in its statement it is aiming to have profits "at the highest level of the worldwide financial industry." It invites comparison as to how it is performing in relation to its competitors. Profit is the yardstick by which it wishes to be measured.

Other companies, too, choose to measure their performance by comparison with other companies in the same field. In a competitive society, companies compete on several levels. They compete for customers, market share, price, and so on. But they also compete for stockholders. It is often important to potential stockholders to consider how a company's profits stack up against those of its competition.

Earlier we mentioned that profits form the basis of the free enterprise system. Because of the close interrelationship between profits and our economic system, a few companies express their support of the free enterprise system in their mission statements.

The Hughes Tool Company for example states, "We believe in the continuation of a free-enterprise system in this country, and hopefully, in the world where people must produce in order to participate in the rewards. We further believe in freedom of political, social, and spiritual systems."

From the preceding we can see that profits play several important roles in mission statements. Putting all of these priorities together in a single statement can be difficult, but most companies find it necessary. In closing, let's look at how some representative companies put profit objectives together:

"Achieving superior results is essential to attract the resources we need to be successful. A long-term commitment to superior profitability is an essential condition for our growth and development as an organization." (Electro Scientific Industries, "Corporate Statement of Purpose")

"We have the responsibility to our shareholders to build business in their behalf. This requires prudent investment in the development of the people, products, and facilities necessary to sustain long-term growth in profits and return on shareholder's investment." (Marion Laboratories "Foundations for an Uncommon Company")

"To attain a continuous high level of profit which places it in the top ranks of industry in its rate of return on invested capital, recognizing that Westinghouse can serve society only if it is financially viable. . . . To achieve steady growth in profits, sales volume and highly productive investment at rates exceeding those of the national economy as a whole. . . . To distribute equitably among owners, employees and customers the fruits of improved productivity and efficient use of management, labor and capital." ("The Westinghouse Purpose")

8

Voting for or against a Company

For many companies the customer plays a vital role in determining its future. The customer determines if the company will ultimately succeed or if it will fail. Although the company may grow big, many feel it can never become too big to remember that its customers have made its growth possible.

Because of the importance of customers, most mission statements have very strong statements concerning them. Perhaps the simplest statement about the customer comes in the Styrotech Corporation's mission statement: "Our company exists primarily to serve the customer."

Another company expressing a similar sentiment is Worthington Industries. Worthington states, "Without the customer and his need for our products and services we have nothing." These companies as well as others have recognized that in our economic system, the customers have a profound impact on who will survive and who will not.

Few companies have the luxury of having a monopoly on a given product or service. Where there is a choice, there is opportunity—the opportunity for the customer to support a company by purchasing its products, and the opportunity for companies to compete for the customer's money.

With each dollar spent, a customer essentially casts a vote. By buying a company's products or services, the customer votes for that company. Similarly, by refusing to buy (or by buying a competitor's product), he casts a vote against that company.

By meeting the needs of the customer better than the competition a company can continue to exist. And by meeting the customer's needs better than anyone else the company can prosper. It is therefore difficult to overestimate the value of a strong base of loyal customers.

Although all industries rely on their customers to provide the money that is their lifeblood, there are certain industries that appear to be more closely aligned with the customer. For the companies in these industries the importance of the customer is magnified, and the mission statements of these companies reflect the increased value of the customer.

Perhaps it is no coincidence that those industries which are the most competitive are the same industries which have the strongest dedication to their customers. As examples, let's look at two highly competitive industries—the retail business and the hotel business.

In the retail industry, where customer attitudes can change rapidly, many successful companies believe they must have their finger on the pulse of the consumer. Knowing the customer is a vital part of the company's success.

For the Super Valu companies, this idea is expressed in "Our Statement of Philosophy." The entire document reflects Super Valu's dedication to its customer, as summed up in a single sentence, "The philosophy of the Super Valu companies will always be a total commitment to serving customers more effectively than anyone else could serve them."

The hotel industry is a second highly competitive industry requiring close ties with its customers. The RHW Hotel Management Company, owners and operators of several Residence Inn Hotels, expresses the commitment to the customer in its mission statement: "We hereby dedicate ourselves and our resources to the provision of total guest satisfaction."

The above industries deal directly with their ultimate customers. They deal with their customers on a one-to-one basis. It is easy to see that for the companies in these industries, the customer is the key to their future.

For other companies who are somewhat farther from their customers, the customer is still very important. Regardless of the distance, it is the customer who decides whether or not to pay for products and services, and this support provides the lifeblood of the corporation's existence. Failure to meet the customer's needs can ultimately mean the failure of the company.

Because of the important role that the customer plays, some companies have not one but several references to the customer in their mission statements. These companies have found it difficult, if not impossible, to mention the importance of the customer in a single sentiment.

At Electro Scientific Industries (ESI), for example, there are three different references to the customer in their "Corporate Statement of Purpose." The first, "Customer satisfaction is what keeps us in business and makes growth possible" shows support for the idea that it is the customer who determines the future of the company. The second, "We must be customer oriented in everything we do" demonstrates the need to keep the customer's needs in mind at all times. The third, "Our products will be judged in terms of our ability to meet our customer's needs" affirms

"If a corporation is to succeed and experience continuing, long-term profitable growth, there must exist a meaningful company philosophy that justifies the personal commitment and dedication of its people."

Jack J. Crocker

September 1973

Our Statement of Philosophy

The philosophy of the Super Valu companies will always be a "total commitment to serving customers more effectively than anyone else could serve them." We believe the pursuit of this meaningful goal is the continuing and overriding responsibility from which every corporate activity must evolve. We value today's success as merely the beginning of a constantly expanding level of achievement.

We believe that customers are most knowledgeable, skilled and capable buyers who will always seek out and do business with that supplier or store which most effectively serves their wants and needs.

Therefore, by serving our customers more effectively than anyone else could serve them, and by efficiently managing our business with highly skilled and dedicated people, we are confident that we shall continue to increase Super Valu's sales and share of market. We believe that this philosophy and practice will result in continuing profitable growth for Super Valu and provide security and opportunity for our many thousands of loyal employees.

Adopted by the Company, January 1974.

Exhibit 34. Super Valu Stores' "Our Statement of Philosophy"

MISSION STATEMENT

RHW Hotel Management Company, Inc.

We hereby dedicate ourselves and
our resources to the provision of
TOTAL GUEST SATISFACTION
for profit, by selecting and developing
individuals within each job classification,
whereby each can best utilize his talents for
self-fulfillment and for the benefit of
our guests....in the form of superior guest service,
an always friendly and helpful environment,
and the cleanest, most comfortable
guest accomodations in our industry.

Exhibit 35. RHW Hotel Management Company's "Mission Statement"

the idea that it is the customer who will be the final judge of the company's products.

Each of these three sentiments is very different, and each is of equal importance. It would be difficult to combine the three sentiments into a single statement. Therefore, ESI has elected to make three separate customer references in its mission statement.

Meeting the customer's needs is often a high priority for many successful companies. For some it is the highest priority, for others it is not. But for all meeting the customer's needs must never be underrated. Failure to recognize the importance of the customer can have disastrous results.

Among the companies that choose the customer as the highest of their priorities is Johnson & Johnson. In "Our Credo" it expresses the idea this way: "We believe our first responsibility is to the doctors, nurses and patients, to mothers and all the others who use our products and services. In meeting their needs everything we do must be of high quality. We must constantly strive to reduce our costs in order to maintain reasonable prices. Customers' orders must be serviced promptly and accurately."

Once a company is successful in meeting customer needs, it is often very important that they continue to meet those needs. Properly servicing the customer is usually not a one-time affair. The successful company must constantly adapt to the customer's needs in order to obtain a steady base of customers. Repeat customers are more valuable than one-time buyers, and it is therefore extremely valuable for companies to be able to build and maintain a steady customer base.

Because of the value of customers, companies must compete with each other in obtaining customer confidence. There is a limited number of customers in existence. Usually some company will meet those needs. It is the most successful companies that can accomplish this better than their competitors.

The Creed of Super Valu...Your Supplier-Partner

We shall so effectively serve our Retailers with both merchandise and services that they may achieve continuing success and a satisfactory growth under all competitive conditions. The future successful growth of Super Valu must always result from our achievement of this meaningful goal.

Since the future success of both Super Valu and our Retailers is relative to, limited by, and dependent upon the future success of each other, there must always exist between us a strong personal bond with mutual responsibilities to each other.

Exhibit 36. Super Valu Stores' "The Creed of Super Valu"

Operating Principles

StorageTek is dedicated to
serving its *Customers* worldwide
by continuing to be the
preferred provider
of high-performance information
storage subsystems, printers, and
supporting services
and by adhering
to the following
principles:

Quality: Our standards of quality will ensure our competitiveness. We will sacrifice short-term gain for reliability and excellence in serving our *Customers'* needs.

Action: Each of us will participate in and contribute to the cost-effective, timely resolution of challenges and opportunities which continuously improve our *Customer* commitment.

People: People are the key to *StorageTek's* success. Individual recognition and advancement will be based upon performance that supports *StorageTek's* commitments to our *Customers* and investors.

Accountability: Our business will be managed to achieve planned growth and long-term profitability. We will grow by building upon demonstrated strengths and meeting *Customers'* needs.

Practices: We will act with integrity to ensure credibility in our relationships with our *Customers,* investors, fellow employees, suppliers and those communities in which we operate worldwide.

StorageTek

Exhibit 37. StorageTek's "Operating Principles"

A part of servicing the customer most effectively is earning their confidence. This sentiment is simply expressed by the Gerber Products Company in their "Objectives": "To deserve and maintain the confidence of those who buy and use our products and services."

It can be a difficult task to earn the confidence of customers. It can involve meeting several diverse goals simultaneously. Each customer is unique, and so too are his or her needs.

A few companies have made specific reference in their mission statements to gaining customer confidence. Such references include providing customers with good value, gaining their trust, providing a quality product, and living up to all commitments made to them. Each of these objectives is discussed below.

The first of these objectives is to provide the customer with good value. "Value" is an abstract term meaning different things to different people. Because of this, Tektronix not only sets the goal to provide good value, they also go on to explain what it is. In its "Statement of Corporate Intent," Tektronix sets this goal: "To provide unmatched value in the product and service we offer customers.... 'Value' is the key word here—a concept that includes not only product usefulness and quality, but also cost."

A second aspect of meeting customers' needs is gaining their trust. A few years ago there was a popular poster featuring a picture of then President Nixon with the caption, "Would you buy a used car from this man?" The same sentiment can be applied to almost any product. Rarely will customers buy from a company they do not trust.

Security Pacific Credo

This Security Pacific Credo is the product of hundreds of employees working to establish a set of ideas which would provide guidelines for decision and action throughout the Corporation. It is clear that among the employees of Security Pacific there are many different definitions of the commitments, obligations and responsibilities of the firm and its employees. This Credo represents much of the collective common ground which exists within the many participants from all levels of the organization who helped bring it to its present stage. It does not represent perfection to any who have participated, but it does represent points of broad general agreement with regard to a desirable collective corporate environment and set of standards for all of us.

The basic objective in developing this Credo was to seek a set of principles and beliefs which might provide guidance and direction to our work, and to continue to build on what we already have. Conflicting pressures in today's highly competitive environment produce different measurements of successes that can accompany economic success. For that reason, we have shaped these six equally important commitments.

COMMITMENT TO THE CUSTOMER

The first commitment is to provide our customers with quality products and services which are innovative and technologically responsive to their current requirements, at appropriate prices. To perform these tasks with integrity requires that we maintain confidentiality and protect customer privacy, promote customer satisfaction and serve customer needs. We strive to serve qualified customers and industries which are socially responsible according to broadly accepted community and company standards.

COMMITMENT TO THE EMPLOYEE

The second commitment is to establish an environment for our employees which promotes professional growth, encourages each person to achieve his or her highest potential, and promotes individual creativity and responsibility. Security Pacific acknowledges our responsibility to employees, including providing for open and honest communication, stated expectations, fair and timely assessment of performance and equitable compensation which rewards employee contribution to company objectives within a framework of equal opportunity and affirmative action.

COMMITMENT OF EMPLOYEE TO SECURITY PACIFIC

The third commitment is that of the employee to Security Pacific. As employees, we strive to understand and adhere to the Corporation's policies and objectives, act in a professional manner, and give our best effort to improve Security Pacific. We recognize the trust and confidence placed in us by our customers and community and act with integrity and honesty in all situations to preserve that trust and confidence. We act responsibly to avoid conflicts of interest and other situations which are potentially harmful to the Corporation.

COMMITMENT OF EMPLOYEE TO EMPLOYEE

The fourth commitment is that of employees to their fellow employees. We must be committed to promote a climate of mutual respect, integrity, and professional relationships, characterized by open and honest communications within and across all levels of the organization. Such a climate will promote attainment of the Corporation's goals and objectives, while leaving room for individual initiative within a competitive environment.

COMMITMENT TO COMMUNITIES

The fifth commitment is that of Security Pacific to the communities which we serve. We must constantly strive to improve the quality of life through our support of community organizations and projects, through encouraging service to the community by employees, and by promoting participation in community services. By the appropriate use of our resources, we work to support or further advance the interests of the community, particularly in times of crisis or social need. The Corporation and its employees are committed to complying fully with each community's laws and regulations.

COMMITMENT TO THE STOCKHOLDER

The sixth commitment of Security Pacific is to its stockholders. We will strive to provide consistent growth and a superior rate of return on their investment, to maintain a position and reputation as a leading financial institution, to protect stockholder investments, and to provide full and timely information. Achievement of these goals for Security Pacific is dependent upon the successful development of the five previous relationships.

Exhibit 38. Security Pacific's Commitments

At Quad/Graphics, trust has a very important role. It is central to corporate philosophy, and in its document entitled, "Trust in Trust at Quad/Graphics," it states its commitment to the customer in this manner: "Customers trust that work will be produced to the most competitive levels of pricing, quality and innovation."

A third aspect, which is crucial to providing good customer relations, is to provide customers with consistently good quality in the products they receive. The commitment to good quality is found throughout many mission statements. One example of this can be found in "Honeywell's Principles," where they state, "Honeywell is dedicated to serving customers through excellence of product, systems and service, and through working together with customers to find the answers to their problems."

The commitment to good quality includes much more than product quality. The commitment includes other aspects as well. References to quality are so pervasive in mission statements that they are covered in more detail in the following chapter.

The final objective involves living up to the commitments made to the customer. Many companies believe that one of the fastest ways to lose the trust of a customer is to fail to deliver what is promised. Once the trust is breached, a customer can be lost forever. Worthington Industries addresses this in their "Philosophy" where they state, "Once a commitment is made to a customer, every effort is made to fulfill that obligation."

There is often an interrelationship that exists between companies and their customers. Both are dependent upon each other to a certain extent. Customers come to rely on companies to supply their needs, and companies rely on customers to create a demand for products. This interrelationship sets up the basis for a partnership.

For the Dow Corning Company, the idea of a partnership with customers is found in its "Code of Business Conduct." In this document, Dow Corning states, "our relationship with each customer is entered in the spirit of a long-term partnership and is predicated on making the customer's interests *our* interests."

The partnership concept applies not only to companies and their customers. It often applies equally to companies and their suppliers. Perhaps this is one of the reasons why companies feel such empathy with their customers. By being customers themselves, the companies have learned to understand the needs of others.

Most companies rely on others to provide the raw materials that are required to make their products. Without high-quality raw materials it would be impossible to produce a high-quality product. This sentiment is expressed simply in "Worthington Industries' Philosophy": "We cannot operate profitably without those who supply the quality raw materials we need for our products."

The concept of partnership between a company and its suppliers is also shown in the mission statement of Electro Scientific Industries. As expressed in its "Corporate Statement of Purpose": "Building mutually beneficial partnerships with our key suppliers is important to our success. To accomplish this relationship, we will share our needs and requirements and endeavor to select suppliers who are willing to work in partnership with us."

Because of the partnership that exists between a company and its suppliers, many companies feel it is the responsibility of a successful company to treat its suppliers equitably. This includes allowing the supplier to make a fair profit. Although companies could probably get their raw materials cheaper, they feel a responsibility to treat their suppliers more equitably.

Two companies expressing this idea in their mission statement are Worthington Industries and Johnson & Johnson: "From a pricing standpoint we ask only that suppliers be competitive in the marketplace and treat us as they do their other customers" ("Worthington Industries' Philosophy"); and "Our suppliers and distributors must have an opportunity to make a fair profit" (Johnson & Johnson, "Our Credo").

As can be seen from the foregoing, the commitment to the customer is a complex one; but it is vital to any company that is to survive. Here are a few passages from mission statements of companies that recognize the importance of the customer.

> "To deliver to customers only products of proven high quality at fair prices and to serve them in such a manner as to earn their continuing respect, confidence and loyalty, both before and after the sale." ("Texaco's Guiding Principles and Objectives")

> "It is our objective to supply to our customers good, reliable products of high value. Shareholders made it possible for us to build our business; our customers make it possible to continue. Our products must satisfy their requirements, our services must meet their needs, and our prices must reflect true value. We intend to maintain a reputation for quality, performance, and reliability. In our dynamic environment, we must anticipate customers' needs and match our new products to their requirements." ("Varian's Objectives and Policies")

> "To fulfill our responsibility to our customers by providing products of high quality incorporating the advances of our technological research and experience, by providing competent sales and service, and by seeking to offer the greatest value by keeping our costs low." ("Hughes Tool Company Corporate and Objectives Philosophy")

> "To customer service. We must excel in meeting the needs of our customers for prompt and efficient service. A Squibb customer must be a satisfied customer." (Squibb Corporation's "Our Commitments")

9

Our Homes

A third element found in many mission statements is the community. There is a special relationship that exists between companies and the communities in which they are located. Each is dependent upon the other. Each gains certain advantages from its association with the other, and each has certain obligations to the other.

Communities benefit from the industries that make their homes there. They provide job opportunities for their citizens, pay taxes to help support the community, and provide financial and other support for community activities. Similarly, corporations derive a benefit from communities that provide a stable work force and services such as hospitals, police and fire protection and for providing their employees with a decent community in which to live.

Many companies believe they have a responsibility to the community and address these in their mission statements. Among the companies who express this responsibility is Ecolab. In their "Quest for Excellence," they simply state, "We recognize the importance of service to society and will contribute positively to the communities in which we operate."

Before addressing how companies support their communities, it might be interesting to consider what constitutes the "community." For a small mom-and-pop enterprise, the community could be the neighborhood in which they are located. A larger company may be interested in the entire city in which it exists. For a multinational company, the community could consist of the entire world. It can easily be seen, therefore, that "community" is a relative term.

For companies that consider their responsibilities to include all of the communities of the world, there is a special challenge. Many of these companies have divisions or subsidiaries located in other countries. These countries may have laws that differ from those of the United States. They may have economic systems with which such companies do not agree. Yet, part of being a responsible citizen of the community requires a company to live within these laws and to support these economic systems. If it cannot tolerate the laws, it must either relocate or work within the legal system to have the laws changed.

To complicate matters further, there is often a difference between where a company actually conducts its business and where it is perceived as conducting its business. One company addressing this concern is the Squibb Corporation. In "Our Commitments," Squibb states, "A business like ours can only prosper if we contribute to the economic health and well-being of the communities in which we do business, and are perceived as doing so." Squibb believes its responsibility goes beyond where it is physically located. It believes it has an equal responsibility to those communities in which it is *perceived* as doing business.

The responsibility to the community is far reaching. It includes such things as bearing one's share of the tax burden, protecting the environment, preserving natural resources, and contributing to worthwhile community programs and events.

The first responsibility a corporation has to the community is to pay its fair share of taxes. This applies to taxes at all levels of government in which the company operates. Federal, state, and local taxes must be paid. While few would say they enjoy paying taxes, many companies recognize the need for doing so, and this is outlined in many mission statements.

Two such companies are Armstrong and Johnson & Johnson. In its "Objectives," Armstrong addresses this issue: "To recognize a basic responsibility to the general public—community, state and nation—and to meet that responsibility by operating a business that contributes to the economic growth and strength of the economy; by providing tax support for necessary government services." In a similar vein, Johnson & Johnson states in "Our Credo," "We must be good citizens—support good works and charities and bear our fair share of taxes."

Another area in which companies state a responsibility to their communities is the environment. Companies recognize that they can have a profound effect, both positive or negative, on the environment. As good citizens, corporations often feel they have a responsibility to protect the natural resources of the community. Achieving this goal is in the best interest of both the community and the corporations located within the community.

Recognizing the value of the environment, many companies make reference to the environment in their mission statements. These tend to fall into two categories. The first is to protect the environment, and the second is to conserve the earth's resources.

The Dow Chemical Company, in its "Objectives," addresses both of these points. In this document Dow sets these objectives: "To share in the world's obligation for the protection of the environment" and "To make wise and efficient use of the earth's energy and natural resources." In a similar sentiment, Honeywell addresses both concerns in a single statement: "Honeywell manages its business in ways that are sensitive to the environment and that conserve natural resources" ("Honeywell Principles").

The third area of responsibility that companies take on is supporting worthwhile community events. This support may be lent any number of ways. The most obvious way to support community activities is through financial contributions to established organizations. Each year corporations are besieged with requests for money for worthy causes. Before contributing, many companies will at least check the organization to assure that it is a legitimate and worthy cause.

Perhaps because it is so time-consuming to analyze each request for funds, some companies have taken steps to assure that the money is distributed equitably. Some will contribute only to a single organization, such as the United Way. This organization will in turn distribute the money as it sees fit. Other companies have separate departments responsible for determining where the money goes. Still other companies set up foundations for this purpose. Regardless of the method of distribution, many large companies contribute vast sums to worthy causes. These contributions are given to charities, research programs, and cultural organizations.

Beyond simple financial contribution, contributing to worthy causes also includes sponsoring activities, setting up organizations to address specific needs, donating assets such as products or buildings, and so on.

Perhaps one of the most important ways for a company to contribute to the community is to encourage its employees to become active participants in community ongoings. By encouraging employee support through the donation of time, there is a mutual benefit for the company, the community, and the employees.

Some companies encourage employees to support activities financially. Support can take the form of financial contributions to a single organization, such as the United Way, or it can include providing matching funds to support educational institutions.

There is a fourth responsibility which a company has to its community which is more subtle than those mentioned above. This responsibility is to be a good citizen of the community. Because there are such strong bonds between a company and its community, the two are often thought of interchangeably. In a community where there is only one industry for example, the character of the town may be the same as the character of the community. Each must rely on the other for earning and maintaining a good name. The reputation that is earned is an asset that is of great benefit to both.

In larger communities hosting a number of industries, the bond may not be as strong, but it is a very real bond. A bankrupt company reflects

THE DOW CHEMICAL COMPANY OBJECTIVES

To seek maximum long-term profit growth as the primary means to ensure the prosperity and well-being of our employees, stockholders and our customers by making products that the people of the world need, and to do so better than anyone else

To attract and hire talented, competent people, and compensate them well for their performance

To provide our employees with opportunities for career growth and decision making

To protect our employees by continuing the development of safe work practices

To continue our commitment to individual freedom and equal opportunity

To practice stewardship in the manufacture, marketing, use and disposal of our products

To share in the world's obligation for the protection of the environment

To make wise and efficient use of the earth's energy and natural resources

To be scrupulously ethical in our daily conduct

To grow through continuous innovation of our products and processes

To be responsible citizens of the different societies in which we operate

To make this world a better place for our having been in business

April, 1979

Exhibit 39. "The Dow Chemical Company Objectives"

Middle South Utilities, Inc.
Corporate Objectives

In fulfilling our public trust as a corporate citizen, Middle South Utilities is firmly committed to these primary objectives:

1. To furnish reliable utility services to customers at the lowest reasonable cost consistent with sound business practices, while continuing to respond to their needs in a courteous and efficient manner.

2. To attain the financial integrity necessary for System companies to provide a fair return to stockholders and to continue serving their customers effectively. Emphasis will be on optimizing capitalization ratios and earning a fair cash return on capital, including that invested in construction, with resultant improved coverages, internal cash generation, and quality of earnings.

3. To seek continual improvement of the work environment within the System to increase productivity, promote safe and efficient operations, encourage employee growth and development, and minimize employee turnover.

4. To be a socially responsible corporate citizen by emphasizing such activities as the social and economic development of our service area and the continuing practice of sound environmental policies consistent with sound business practices.

5. To pursue active marketing plans which will encourage the efficient use of electrical energy, increase profitable sales that will produce economic advantages to our service area and System companies and promote the development and application of innovative energy technologies which are economic to the customer and provide a fair return on investment.

6. To effectively communicate through interaction with various publics on matters involving or relating to the System companies, their programs and actions, so as to build understanding and assure appropriate meeting of customer needs.

Exhibit 40. Middle South Utilities' "Corporate Objectives"

negatively on the entire community. Similarly, a company that moves from one city to another has the same effect. A few years ago, the Brooklyn Dodgers moved their operations to Los Angeles. Many people in Brooklyn have never forgiven them for that. Although they have long been disassociated with Brooklyn, many still refer to the Dodgers as the "Brooklyn Bums."

It is important for a company to earn a good reputation, and part of doing this is to conduct its business in an ethical manner. Most companies have a code of ethics separate from their mission statements. Perhaps for this reason many companies do not mention ethics in their mission statements.

A code of ethics, whether written or understood is important to virtually every company. There are a few companies that find them important enough to reiterate in their mission statements. Two such companies are the Dana Corporation and Worthington Industries. They state, "The Dana Corporation will be a good citizen worldwide. We will do business in a professional and ethical manner" (Dana's "Policies"), and "Worthington Industries practices good citizenship at all levels. We conduct our business in a professional and ethical manner when dealing with customers, neighbors and the general public worldwide" ("Worthington Industries' Philosophy").

At the beginning of this chapter we mentioned a larger community, to which we all belong, and that is the community of the entire world. One company recognizing this sets a rather noble goal. The Dow Chemical Company sets this as one of its "Objectives": "To make this world a better place for our having been in business." Accomplishing this task could be the noblest task of any enterprise.

In summarizing this chapter let's look at how some corporations express their commitments to the communities in which they operate:

> "We believe we are obligated to be responsible in conducting the affairs of the Sun Company to the interests of its customers, employees and stockholders. Also, we must be responsible to the broader concerns of the public, including especially the general desire for improvement in the quality of life, equal opportunity for all, and the constructive use of natural resources." (Sun Company, "The Creed We Work By")

> "We are responsible to the communities in which we live and work and to the world community as well. We must be good citizens— support good works and charities and bear our fair share of taxes. We must encourage civic improvements and better health education. We must maintain in good order the property we are privileged to use, protecting the environment and natural resources." (Johnson & Johnson's "Our Credo")

"To recognize a basic responsibility to the general public—community, state and nation—and to meet that responsibility by operating a business that contributes to the economic growth and strength of the economy; by providing tax support for necessary government service; by aiding worthy health, educational, and welfare institutions; by taking an active part in our community affairs; and by participating in the formulation of sound public policy directed to the achievement of a social and economic climate favorable to growth, prosperity, high employment, and national well-being." (Armstrong's "Principles and Objectives")

"Our company will behave as a good citizen and a good neighbor in every community in which it operates. We will be aware of national goals in each country and support generally accepted community objectives." (Varian's "Objectives and Policies")

10

Reaching for
the Top

Another element quite commonly found in mission statements is a commitment to high quality. More and more companies are recognizing the need to provide their customers with quality in the products and services they produce. While there certainly are companies who fail in delivering quality, many of the most successful companies have tried to make it a requirement.

Often companies rely on customers to make multiple purchases. It is the repeat customer who helps the company achieve its sales objective. To earn a repeat customer, the company must provide that customer with a quality product at a competitive price. Failing to deliver the quality in one product can lose a customer—and his or her repeat purchases—for life.

In a competitive society meeting the needs of the customers is important. Failure to do so opens the door for competitive pressures. Recognizing this, many companies have placed quality high on the list of priorities in company philosophy and mission statements.

An aspect that is closely associated with the commitment to quality is a commitment to excellence. The word excellence has become even more of a buzzword in corporate language recently. Perhaps this is because of the popularity of such books as *In Search of Excellence* and *A Passion for Excellence*. Whatever the reason, the themes of quality and excellence are repeated often in many mission statements. Although quality and excellence are closely associated with each other, we will look at them separately. Then we will see how they can be tied together.

In an attempt to promote their quality image, some companies have used advertising slogans. These slogans are an effort to promote their names as synonymous with quality. Two of the more successful slogans are, "The quality goes in before the name goes on" and "Quality is job one." Most

Corning Glass Works Quality Statement

GOAL

To make Corning Glass Works a leader in delivering error-free products and services, on time, that meet customer requirements 100% of the time.

POLICY

It is the policy of Corning Glass Works to achieve Total Quality performance in meeting the requirements of external and internal customers. Total Quality performance means understanding who the customer is, what the requirements are, and meeting those requirements, without error, on time, every time.

DEFINITION OF QUALITY

Quality is knowing what needs to be done, having the tools to do it right, then doing it right—the first time.

IMPLEMENTATION

It is intended that every employee be taught what Total Quality is and why it is necessary to attain it. Each employee will be trained in how to achieve Total Quality in his or her job and given the tools to do the job right the first time. Management will provide the resources, structure and atmosphere that will allow and encourage individuals and groups to meet the Total Quality goal and policy. While responsibility for achieving the goal must ultimately rest with management, the actions required to realize Total Quality rest with each employee of the company.

Exhibit 41. "Corning Glass Works Quality Statement"

people can easily recognize these slogans without hearing the company name.

With mission statements, too, companies attempt to equate their name with a quality image. The quality image is necessary to insure the company's continued existence. In its "Operating Principles," StorageTek explains the importance of quality in this manner: "Our standards of quality will ensure our competitiveness."

For some companies the commitment to quality is the company's highest priority. For the Ford Motor Company, this sentiment is expressed both in its advertising—"Quality is job one"—and in its mission statement: "Quality comes first—To achieve customer satisfaction, the quality of our products and services must be our number one priority." By assuring the highest quality product is produced, everybody becomes a winner: the customer gets better value in the product purchased; the company gains a reputation that will help it obtain repeat business; and, finally, the employees gain the satisfaction of meeting customer needs better than anyone else.

When a customer purchases a product, he shows support for the company that supplies the product. It is therefore in the best interest of the company to provide products of high quality. This applies not only to the company, but to its employees, and to the society in which they live. This sentiment is simply expressed in "Foundations for an Uncommon Company" at Marion Laboratories. In this document Marion states, "We have a special responsibility to our associates, our customers, and to society to provide products and service of the highest quality and to conduct our business with integrity and the highest ethical standards."

Similar to the goal of obtaining high quality is the commitment to excellence. The two are so closely related that often they are interchangeable. By achieving high quality and by constantly improving on that high quality, excellence can be achieved. One company that ties these goals together in this manner is Honeywell. In their "Principles" Honeywell explains this concept as follows: "Quality of product, application and service is essential to continue Honeywell's success. Quality improvement should pervade every job within the company. Honeywell believes quality results from an environment in which people work together to sustain excellence."

Quality is often considered a responsibility. This is also the case with excellence. This idea is reflected in the following statement, again from Marion Laboratories' "Foundations for an Uncommon Company": "We have a responsibility for excellence and innovation. . . . We do all that we do to the very best of our ability and with the strongest enthusiasm we can generate. It is the very nature of our business to do things that have never been done before and for which there are always reasons they cannot be done. Success for us requires the ability and the spirit to find a pathway through any obstacle, even when no pathway is visible at the start."

It should be pointed out that excellence goes beyond just product excellence. It applies equally well to all other phases of business. While many companies express a commitment to excellence, few go to the lengths to which the Squibb Corporation goes. The theme of excellence is found throughout its "Commitments." Here Squibb sets the goal of achieving excellence in science and innovation, in product, and in management. The following are some excerpts from this document addressing each of these areas:

> "Squibb science must be, and be perceived to be, of world class stature in each of our areas of specialization in terms of basic biomedical research, product formulations and clinical research. All of our operations must excel in terms of their respective technologies and in terms of product innovation. Squibb will not enter, or remain in a field in which it cannot technologically excel."

> "To product excellence. All of our products must be top quality, deliver the benefits they promise and be cost effective. The 'Priceless Ingredient' is as priceless as ever."

> "To excellence in management. By this we mean: an open and participatory management style with employees at all levels being encouraged to contribute to the decision-making process; the fewest possible layers of management; timely decision making at the lowest appropriate responsibility level; state-of-the-art management information systems; and the highest degree of competence and professionalism at all levels of the organization."

General Signal is another company that recognizes that excellence applies to aspects beyond product excellence. In its credo, it sums this up simply by expressing "A commitment to excellence in every aspect of our business."

As the above passages show, the commitment to excellence is common in all aspects of business. By striving for excellence in all things done, companies believe they will best serve the interest of their customers, the public, their employees, and themselves.

As we have seen, obtaining the highest possible quality and striving for excellence in all phases of business are two goals common to many companies. These two goals seem to form a common backbone in mission statements. Perhaps this should not be surprising when you consider what a mission statement is actually intended to accomplish. In its mission statement a company articulates what it *strives* to achieve. It sets goals for itself and tells those who read it what it considers important. Like all successful enterprises, striving to be the best is the best way of doing business. By the same token, setting low goals would be of little or no value to anyone.

Many believe that achieving excellence in any aspect of business is a never-ending process. No matter how well a company does its job, there is always room for additional improvement. Being the best may not be good enough. It is also important to make the best even better. As the English Statesman Oliver Cromwell said in the 17th century, "He who stops being better stops being good." This sentiment is expressed at the Gerber Products Company in their "Corporate Mission": "To strive in all things, and with all people, to do the best we can and to make our best better."

There is a separate document in which Gerber Products sets for itself an admirable goal. One of its objectives is "To deserve and maintain the confidence of those who buy and use our products." Gerber's products are sold in a market where customers place a great deal of trust in the quality of the product. Perhaps this is the reason it is so essential for Gerber to keep improving on its best.

As we have seen, the goals of quality and excellence are common to the mission statements of many companies. In summarizing this chapter, let's examine how some companies have expressed their commitments to these two objectives.

Ecolab's Quest for Excellence
Our Mission, Philosophy, and
Standards of Performance

OUR MISSION

Our business is to be a leading innovator, developer and marketer of global services, specialty products and systems, which provide superior value to our customers while conserving resources and preserving the quality of the environment and providing a fair profit for our shareholders.

OUR SHAREHOLDERS

We will be a growth company. We will provide our shareholders with a 15% annual growth in per share earnings while continually investing in product research and business development to assure a reliable future. Dividends will be consistent and recognize shareholders' needs for an adequate return and the company's need for growth capital. Our financial objectives also include a minimum 20% return on beginning of the year shareholders' equity and an "A" rated balance sheet.

EMPLOYEES

We are dedicated to the belief that the most important resource is people who respond positively to recognition, involvement and opportunities for personal and career development. We are most productive and fulfilled in an environment where we empower and are empowered to act. We will address problems and mistakes constructively, learn from them and contribute to their solution. We encourage a team approach with mutually supportive relationships based on objectivity, integrity, openness and trust.

OUR CUSTOMERS

The company that fails its customers, fails! We will be superior to our competitors in providing the highest value to our customers at a fair price. We will constantly listen to our customers, respond quickly to their current needs and anticipate future needs.

OUR ORGANIZATION

We seek an organization that is flexible, innovative, responsive and entrepreneurial. To accomplish this, we will create decentralized business units which have great freedom, within corporate strategy and policy limits, to develop their own business strategies and plans and to achieve agreed upon objectives. Actions will be judged on the extent to which they promote the overall good of the corporation over the separate interests of groups.

OUR SOCIETY

We recognize the importance of service to society and will contribute positively to the communities in which we operate. Our company's business will be conducted in accordance with the law and stated corporate and societal standards of conduct.

Exhibit 42. "Ecolab's Quest for Excellence"

OUR COMMITMENTS

We, in Squibb, are committed to these values:

To increasing shareholders' value. We seek to maximize total return on investment for our shareholders in terms of capital appreciation and current income by gradually increasing both investment in the business and dividends.

To excellence in science and innovation. Squibb science must be, and be perceived to be, of world class stature in each of our areas of specialization in terms of basic biomedical research, product formulations and clinical research. All of our operations must excel in terms of their respective technologies and in terms of product innovation. Squibb will not enter, or remain in, a field in which it cannot technologically excel.

To product excellence. All of our products must be of top quality, deliver the benefits they promise and be cost effective. The "Priceless Ingredient" is as priceless as ever.

To customer service. We must excel in meeting the needs of our customers for prompt and efficient service. A Squibb customer must be a satisfied customer.

To excellence in management. By this we mean: an open and participatory management style with employees at all levels being encouraged to contribute to the decision-making process; the fewest possible layers of management; timely decision making at the lowest appropriate responsibility level; state of the art management information systems; and the highest degree of competence and professionalism at all levels of the organization.

To management development. Far more than plant, property and equipment, our human resources are our most valuable assets. We are committed to developing the skills of our people at all levels of the organization. Management development, career planning and succession planning are at the core of our operating philosophy.

To concern for people. We shall promote a feeling of teamwork and mutual self-respect among all employees, and provide opportunities for all our employees to grow professionally and personally. We shall maintain an attractive and supportive work environment contributing to employee well-being and job effectiveness. We shall encourage and reward superior performance, initiative and innovation.

To social responsibility. A business like ours can only prosper if we contribute to the economic health and well-being of the communities in which we do business, and are perceived as doing so.

"The Priceless Ingredient of every product is the honor and integrity of its maker."™

Exhibit 43. Squibb Corporation's "Our Commitments"

"Continuous improvement is essential to our success—we must strive for excellence in everything we do: in our products, in their safety and value—and in our services, our human relations, our competitiveness, and our profitability. Integrity is never compromised—The conduct of our company worldwide must be pursued in a manner that is socially responsible and commands respect for its integrity and for its positive contributions to society. Our doors are open to men and women alike without discrimination and without regard to ethnic origin or personal beliefs." (Ford Motor Company's "Company Mission, Values, and Guiding Principles")

"Our reputation, established on honesty and quality, is a heritage we treasure and must continue to earn every day. We commit ourselves and pledge our resources to the continued quest for excellence so that future generations may also recognize and rely upon the integrity of Gerber Products Company." (Gerber Products Company's "Corporate Mission")

"We will set the highest performance standards for both individuals and business units; invest in our people and help them develop the knowledge and skills necessary to meet these standards; demand performance consistent with such standards; and reward our people in accordance with those standards. We will achieve our goals through a dedication to quality, integrity, and excellence in everything we do. This will be clearly visible in the commitment and care we extend to our shareholders, our customers, and our people." ("Chase Vision")

11

The Personality of the Mission Statement

A mission statement, in a sense, represents the personality of a company. It expresses positive attributes about the company and its employees. By developing certain positive personality traits in its people, a company can share in the positive reputation fostered by such traits.

Like all organizations, companies are made up of people, and it is people that give each company its own unique personality. Often, the kind of personality traits that make people "good people," are the same kinds of traits that make companies "good companies." In their mission statements, many companies stress positive personality traits they hope to instill in their people.

Perhaps the most recognizable personality trait expressed in mission statements is the "Golden Rule." This idea, which is familiar to almost everyone, is included in the mission statements of many companies. Two examples are shown below. The first is found in the "Foundations for an Uncommon Company" by Marion Laboratories. The second is from "Worthington Industries' Philosophy."

"We should treat others as we would be treated . . . with dignity, respect, integrity and honesty. This applies to:
Associates and their families
Customers
     Consumers
     Health Care Providers
     Wholesalers
Stockholders
Suppliers
Financial Community & General Public"

"We treat customers, employees, investors and suppliers as we would like to be treated."

The Golden Rule expresses an idea that is timeless. There are few people who are unfamiliar with this idea; it is a significant tenet of three of the world's major religions. Although it is quite old, many companies find it is as appropriate today as ever.

Many of the personality traits discussed in mission statements are the kinds of things one would logically expect. They include such things as trust, honor, integrity, ethics, hard work, and honesty. Traits such as these are the building blocks upon which companies hope to earn good reputations.

The first of these traits is trust. When customers purchase products they are placing their trust in the manufacturer of that product. Rarely will anyone make a purchase from a company or person they distrust. Trust is important in all aspects of business. Just as customers must trust a company, so too must the employees of a company place their trust in those with whom they work. The mission statement of Quad/Graphics shows that trust is a key aspect in all areas of its business. In this document, entitled "Trust in Trust at Quad/Graphics," the company expresses the importance of trust in each of five areas: teamwork, responsibility, productivity, the management, and "think small."

Two other companies who highlight trust in their missions are Ford Motor Company and the Sun Company. From Ford's "Company Mission, Values, and Guiding Principles," we find this sentiment: "We are a team. We must treat each other with trust and respect." And from Sun Company's "The Creed We Work By" we find, "We believe that managers of organizations hold a trust, and that their stewardship demands scrupulous treatment of the loyalties and resources committed to their direction. We acknowledge this principle as it applies specifically to us."

While most companies want to be trusted, trustworthiness is an earned trait. There are many ways of earning trust, one is by conducting business with honor and integrity. The Squibb Corporation has an interesting little story that provides insight about these traits. While not a mission statement per se, "The Priceless Ingredient" tells the story of a young man who seeks to receive the most for what he spends. He is told to look for the Priceless Ingredient: "the Priceless Ingredient of every product is the honor and integrity of its maker. Consider his name before you buy."

Like Squibb, many companies place a high value on integrity, and many include these thoughts in their mission statement. Some references to the importance of integrity include these:

"Integrity is never compromised—The conduct of our Company worldwide must be pursued in a manner that is socially responsible and commands respect for its integrity and for its positive contributions to society. Our doors are open to men and women alike without discrimination and without regard to ethnic origin or per-

TRUST IN TRUST
AT QUAD/GRAPHICS

The Trust of Teamwork. Employees trust that together they will do better than as individuals apart.

The Trust of Responsibility. Employers trust that each will carry his/her fair share of the load.

The Trust in Productivity. Customers trust that work will be produced to the most competitive levels of pricing, quality and innovation.

The Trust of Management. Shareholders, customers and employees that trust the company will make decisive judgements for the long-term rather than the short-term goals or today's profit.

The Trust of Think-Small. We all trust in each other: we regard each other as persons of equal rank; we respect the dignity of the individual by recognizing not only the individual accomplishments, but the feelings and needs of the individual and family as well; and we all share the same goals and purpose in life.

QuadGraphics

Exhibit 44. "Trust in Trust at Quad/Graphics"

Celestial Seasonings' Beliefs

EXCELLENCE

We believe that in order to make this world a better place in which to live, we must be totally dedicated to the endless quest for excellence in the important tasks which we endeavor to accomplish.

OUR PRODUCTS

We believe in marketing and selling healthful and naturally oriented products that nurture people's bodies and uplift their souls. Our products must be superior in quality, a good value, beautifully artistic, and philosophically inspiring.

OUR GROWTH

We believe in aggressive, steady, predictable, and well-planned growth in sales and earnings. We are intent on building a large company that will flourish into the next century.

DIGNITY OF THE INDIVIDUAL

We believe in the dignity of the individual, and we are totally committed to the fair, honest, kind, and professional treatment of all individuals and organizations with whom we work.

OUR EMPLOYEES

We believe that our employees develop a commitment to excellence when they are directly involved in the management of their areas of responsibility. This team effort maximizes quality results, minimizes costs, and allows our employees the opportunity to have authorship and integrity in their accomplishments, as well as sharing in the financial rewards of their individual and team efforts.

We believe in hiring above-average people who are willing to work for excellent results. In exchange, we are committed to the development of our good people by identifying, cultivating, training, rewarding, retaining, and promoting those individuals who are committed to moving our organization forward.

OUR ENVIRONMENT

We believe in fostering an environment which promotes creativity and encourages possibility thinking throughout the organization. We plan our work to be satisfying, productive, and challenging. As such, we support an atmosphere which encourages intelligent risk-taking without the fear of failure.

OUR DREAM

Our role at Celestial Seasonings is to play an active part in making this world a better place by unselfishly serving the public. We believe we can have a significant impact on making people's lives happier and healthier through their use of our products. By dedicating our total resources to this dream, everyone profits: our customers, consumers, employees, and shareholders.

Exhibit 45. Celestial Seasonings' Statement of Beliefs

---

sonal beliefs." (Ford Motor Company's "Company Mission, Values, and Guiding Principles")

"Our reputation is one of our most valued assets. We will conduct our business in sound ethical principles based on integrity and fairness to all our constituencies." (Ferro Corporation's "Broad Statement of Mission")

"Honeywell believes in the highest level of integrity and ethical behavior in relationships with customers, employees, shareholders, vendors, neighbors and governments." ("Honeywell Principles")

As can be seen in the above passages, there is a close tie-in between "integrity" and "ethics." The two concepts are similar. In a previous chapter it was mentioned that to be good citizens of a community, corporations had to act in an ethical manner. Employees, too, are expected to behave ethically. Employees serve as representatives of their company, and when their actions are below par, it reflects negatively on their employer.

Many companies have codes of ethics which are separate from their mission statements. More often than not, new employees must sign this document as a condition of employment. This type of practice demonstrates the importance of ethics. Often the penalty for violating the code of ethics is severe: up to and including dismissal.

Another trait frequently expressed in mission statements is hard work, as illustrated in the "Worthington Industries' Philosophy": "From employees we expect an honest day's work for an honest day's pay," and Hughes Tool Company's "Corporate Objectives and Philosophy": "We believe that all work is dignified, to get the most from life, one must WORK HARD and toward realistic OBJECTIVES."

The company which asks its employees for honest, hard work is making a reasonable request. Corporations make a substantial commitment by hiring people to work for them. They deserve an honest effort from people in their employ.

A key aspect of corporate functioning expressed in mission statements is communication. It is important for the communication to be a two-way street. It is important for the management to communicate with their constituents to keep them aware and informed. Likewise, it is important for the employees to communicate with their management. A few companies point these ideas out in their mission statements.

The idea that management, because it is ultimately responsible for the success or failure of a company, must fully communicate with its constituents is documented in the "Worthington Industries' Philosophy" as follows: "We communicate through every possible channel with our customers, employees, shareholders, and financial community."

The other side of communication falls on the hands of the employees. They provide the information on which the management bases its decisions. It is therefore important that they communicate with their upper management. This is simply summed up in the "Statement of Corporate Intent" of the Hershey Foods Corporation: "To successfully conduct the business of the Corporation, it is necessary that each employee strive to improve the communications relating to his or her area of responsibility."

In the preceding paragraphs, we have discussed several personality traits found in mission statements. By instilling these ideals in their employees, the company goes a long way in earning a valuable asset: a good reputation. A reputation is not something that can be bought or sold; it must be earned. Once earned, it is important that steps be taken to preserve that good name.

The Goodyear Tire and Rubber Company has a very simple credo that reflects this attitude: "Protect Our Good Name." This creed was originally adopted in 1915 and is essentially the basis for the company's social responsiveness in succeeding years. For over seventy years this creed has been used by Goodyear. Although many things have changed over the years, the value of this idea has not. In commenting about the value of the creed in today's world, the Chairman of Goodyear had this to say, "we feel that our creed 'Protect Our Good Name' is more relevant and more valuable than ever before, as both a discipline and an inspiration."

The Gerber Products Company has a similar idea expressed in its "Corporate Mission." Here it states, "Our reputation, established on honesty

ADOLPH COORS COMPANY AND SUBSIDIARIES

Corporate Code of Conduct

Throughout its history of growth and technological achievement, Adolph Coors Company and subsidiaries (hereinafter Coors Industries) have been characterized by a work environment that encourages both teamwork and individual initiative—two key elements of the free enterprise system. It has been recognized, however, that individual freedom and creativity exist within a framework of ethical and legal considerations. This code, while not all inclusive, is intended to define this longstanding framework to guide the productive energy of each employee of Coors Industries.

CORPORATE PHILOSOPHY

Product Quality. Coors Industries will develop, produce and sell products of recognizably superior quality at competitive prices.

Community Affairs. Coors Industries shall be involved in the affairs of the communities in which it conducts business or in which its employees reside. It will actively support worthwhile community programs through financial contributions consistent with available resources. It will also encourage individual participation in community activities by all employees.

Equal Employment Opportunity. Coors Industries will provide equal opportunity in employment to all individuals without regard to race, creed, color, sex, sexual preference, age, handicap or national origin.

Working Environment, Safety and Health. Coors Industries will conduct its business in such a manner that employees, potential employees and the community will consider it a desirable employer for which to work. Wages, salaries and benefits will be competitive. A work environment that demands excellence and rewards accomplishment. Operations will be conducted with the highest regard for employee health and safety

EMPLOYEE CONDUCT

Conduct of Business. Whenever Coors' Industries does business, its employees or its representatives will conduct themselves in accordance with applicable United States laws as well as with local laws, customs and traditions. Company employees or representatives will make no payments to obtain special treatment. No employee or representative will encourage other employees, distributors, suppliers or any customer of Coors products to violate any law in order to maintain or gain business for Coors Industries.

Conflicts of Interest. No employee or representative will maintain outside interests, either personal or financial, which are in conflict with duties or responsibilities as a Company employee or representative.

Confidential Information. Employees shall not discuss confidential Company affairs with other employees except on a "need to know" basis. Employees in possession of confidential information must refrain from disclosing it to anyone outside the Company, and must not trade in Coors stock until there has been full public disclosure of such information through properly authorized channels. An employee must refrain from recommending the purchase, sale or holding of Coors stock in any circumstance.

Contributions. Coors Industries may make political, civic or charitable contributions in states or countries when permitted by law, but only as authorized by Adolph Coors Company's Board of Directors.

Corporate Hospitality Toward Public Officials. Hospitality toward public officials shall be of such a scale and nature as to avoid compromising the integrity or impugning the reputation of the public official or the Company. All such acts should be performed in the expectation that they will become a matter of public knowledge.

Proper Accounting. Compliance with accepted accounting rules and control is expected of Coors Industries, its officers and employees at all times. Accounting and control systems will be maintained which are adequate to provide reasonable assurance that assets are safeguarded from loss or unauthorized use and which produce records adequate for preparation of reliable financial information. No payment on behalf of Coors Industries shall be approved or made with the intention or understanding that a part or all of such payment is to be used for any purpose other than that described by the documents supporting the payment.

Reporting Compliance. All employees of Coors Industries are responsible for monitoring and enforcement within their specific areas of responsibility.

Discovery by any employee of any event which is in violation of the foregoing policies is to be reported immediately to the Senior Vice President of Finance or the President of Adolph Coors Company. Reported violations will be formally and immediately acknowledged.

Annually, at year end, each officer, director and manager shall prepare a letter for submission to the Senior Vice President of Finance which shall affirm a knowledge and understanding of this Code and shall report any transactions or events in which it appears the foregoing policies are not being observed. These statements will in turn be reviewed by the Audit Committee.

Violation of Code. Willful violation of the Employee Conduct section of this Code is grounds for disciplinary action, up to, and including, dismissal.

Exhibit 46. Adolph Coors Company and Subsidiaries' "Corporate Code of Conduct"

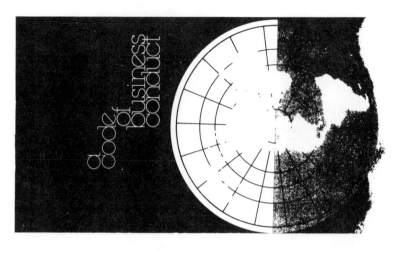

a Code of business conduct

DOW CORNING CORPORATION

To Dow Corning Employees:

This is the fourth edition of the Code of Conduct. Since it was first published in 1976, business conditions around the world have been changing at a rapid pace. At the same time our business has continued to grow and has also become more challenging and complex. Through it all, you — the people of this company — have continued to practice our long-held belief that business and society are best served through actions based on fair, legal and ethical principles.

The Code of Conduct is a part of a larger set of Dow Corning Values that apply to all employees in all of our operations. Each Value is of equal importance and, together, they are interdependent. These are the Values that characterize Dow Corning:

INTEGRITY. Our integrity is demonstrated in our ethical conduct and in our respect for the values cherished by the society of which we are a part.

EMPLOYEES. Our employees are the source from which our ideas, actions and performance flow. The full potential of our people is best realized in an environment that breeds fairness, self-fulfillment, teamwork and dedication to excellence.

CUSTOMERS. Our relationship with each customer is entered in the spirit of a long-term partnership and is predicated on making the customer's interests our interests.

QUALITY. Our never-ending quest for quality performance is based on our understanding of our customer's needs and our willingness and capability to fulfill those needs.

TECHNOLOGY. Our advancement of chemistry and related sciences in our chosen fields is the Value that most differentiates Dow Corning.

SAFETY. Our attention to safety is based on our full time commitment to injury free work, individual self-worth and a consideration for the well being of others.

PROFIT. Our long-term profit growth is essential to our long-term existence. How our profits are derived, and the purposes for which they are used, are influenced by our Values and our shareholders.

If these Values, or beliefs, seem familiar to you, they should; most have been a part of Dow Corning for decades. Our commitment to quality improvement and our emphasis on partnerships with customers have received special attention in recent years. Our Values are what we all, as members of the Dow Corning team, have in common. Let's always keep them in the forefront.

John S. Ludington

John S. Ludington
Chairman and Chief Executive

Dow Corning
Area Headquarters

United States
Midland Center
P.O. Box 1767
Midland, MI 48640

Europe
154 Chaussee de la Hulpe
1170 Brussels, Belgium

Inter-America
Midland Center
P.O. Box 1767
Midland, MI 48640

Pacific
4 Ray Road
Epping
New South Wales 121 Australia

Japan
15-1, Nishi Shimbashi 1-chome
Minato-Ku, Tokyo, 105, Japan

Dow Corning Corporation
Midland, Michigan 48640 U.S.A.

Integrity: A Basic Dow Corning Value

Among those values that characterize Dow Corning is integrity. A key element in maintaining our corporate integrity is fair, legal and ethical business practice. Our business practice is determined by the individual decisions and actions of each Dow Corning employee. The Code of Conduct addresses several, but not all, important issues and situations. Those not covered are expected to be resolved through the sound judgment of each employee, discussion with your manager or, as needed, review with the Business Conduct Committee.

Dow Corning's Responsibilities to Employees:

All relations with employees will be guided by our belief that the dignity of the individual is primary.

Opportunity without bias will be afforded each employee in relation to demonstrated ability, initiative and potential.

Management practices will be consistent with our intent to provide employment stability and opportunity for all productive employees.

Qualified citizens of countries where we do business will be hired and trained for available positions consistent with their capabilities.

The work environment will encourage individual self-fulfillment, the maximization of skills and talents, open communication and the free exchange of information and ideas.

A safe, clean and pleasant work environment that at minimum meets all applicable laws and regulations will be provided.

The privacy of an individual's personal records will be respected; employees may participate in a review of their personnel records upon request.

Employee's Responsibilities to Dow Corning:

Proprietary information is a highly valued corporate asset that, if lost or negligently disclosed, could be detrimental to Dow Corning's interests. Employees will protect information about our business activities, plans and technology as well as other sensitive information. The proprietary information of others will not be obtained by using illegal or unethical methods. Customer information, when made available to employees, will be handled with the utmost discretion.

Employees must be free of conflicting interests which could inhibit or detract from their on-the-job performance or with Dow Corning's business interests

© 1987 Dow Corning Corporation

Employees will not engage in bribery, price fixing, kickbacks, collusion, or any practice which might give the appearance of being illegal or unethical.

Employees will avoid discussions with competitors that could be construed as unfair competition or the restriction of free trade. Relations with competitors will be limited to buyer-seller agreements, licensing agreements or matters of general concern to the industry or society. All such discussions will be documented.

Relations with Customers, Distributors, Suppliers:

Dow Corning is committed to providing products and services that meet the requirements of our customers. We will provide information and support necessary to maximize the use and effectiveness of our products.

Dow Corning will regularly encourage its distributors, agents, representatives and other parties who represent Dow Corning to conduct their business on our behalf in a legal and ethical manner. Business integrity is a criterion for the selection and retention of those who represent Dow Corning.

The purchase of supplies, materials and services will be based on quality, price, service, ability to supply and the vendor's adherence to legal and ethical business practices. Fees paid for business services must be reasonable and in line with customary local rates.

Conservation, Environmental, Product Stewardship and Social Responsibilities:

Dow Corning will be responsible for the impact of its technology upon the environment. We will protect the natural environment by continually seeking reasonable ways to eliminate or minimize discharges of potentially harmful waste materials.

All waste will be recycled when possible and economical. Non-recyclable waste will be disposed of in accordance with applicable standards.

New facilities will be designed to optimize the efficient use of natural resources and to conserve energy. Existing facilities will be modified to meet current and anticipated environmental laws and regulations.

We will continually strive to assure that our products and services are safe, efficacious and accurately represented in our literature, advertising and package identification.

Product characteristics, including toxicity and potential hazards, will be made known to those who produce, package, transport, use and dispose of Dow Corning products.

Dow Corning will build and maintain positive relationships with communities where we have a presence. Our efforts will focus on education, civic, cultural and health and safety programs.

International Business Guidelines:

Dow Corning endeavors to be a productive and cooperative corporate citizen wherever we do business. We recognize, however, that laws, business practices and customs differ from country to country and may occasionally inhibit rather than foster open competition. If there is a conflict with U.S. law or a Dow Corning standard of business conduct, we will seek reasonable ways to resolve the difference. Failing resolution, Dow Corning will remove itself from the particular business situation.

Dow Corning personnel will not authorize or give payments or gifts to government employees or their beneficiaries in order to obtain or retain business. We will strongly discourage facilitating payments to expedite the performance of routine services. Where the practice is common and there is no reasonable alternative, a minimum payment may be considered. Such payments will be accurately documented and recorded.

No payment, contribution or service will be offered by Dow Corning to a political party or a candidate, even in countries where such payments are legal.

While encouraging the transborder transfer of technology necessary to support its subsidiaries and joint ventures, Dow Corning expects to receive fair compensation for, and protection of, its technology.

Dow Corning will strive to establish intercompany prices at a level that would prevail in arm's length transactions. The intent of this approach to pricing is to assure each country a fair valuation of goods and services transferred.

Financial Responsibilities:

Dow Corning funds will be used only for purposes that are legal and ethical. All transactions will be properly and accurately recorded.

Dow Corning will maintain a system of internal accounting controls and assure that all involved employees are fully apprised of that system.

Dow Corning encourages the free flow of funds for investment, borrowing, dividending and the return of capital throughout the world.

We Are Committed . . .

. . . to the letter and spirit of this Code of Business Conduct. The character and conduct of Dow Corning Corporation depend on the actions of its employees. As a Dow Corning employee, you are expected to know these standards and live up to them.

Exhibit 47. Dow Corning Company's Code of Conduct

Gerber Products Company
Corporate Mission

The people and resources of Gerber Products Company and its affiliated companies are dedicated to providing quality products and services at reasonable prices, and to meeting the needs of our customers in a responsible and responsive manner as we have for more than three generations.

Corporate Management will provide strategic planning and direction to:

◊ maintain our position of leadership in the marketplace

◊ maintain our recognition as an authority in the field of infant health, nutrition, and care

◊ grow through aggressive consumer marketing and sound diversification and acquisitions

◊ protect and increase the value of our shareholders' investments.

We strive to meet our social responsibilities and to improve the quality of life for our customers, our communities, our shareholders, and our employees.

Our reputation, established on honesty and quality, is a heritage we treasure and must continue to earn every day. We commit ourselves and pledge our resources to the continued quest for excellence so that future generations may also recognize and rely upon the integrity of Gerber Products Company.

Exhibit 48. Gerber Products Company's "Corporate Mission"

Gerber Products Company
Objectives are...

.. To offer needed, quality products and services at reasonable prices for families with infants and small children.

.. To deserve and maintain the confidence of those who buy and use our products and services.

.. To maintain an organization of which all employees may be proud, and upon which they can depend for fair and consistent management and sound business decisions.

.. To serve actively as good corporate citizens in all communities where we live and work.

.. To strive in all things, and with all people, to do the best we can and to make our best better.

Exhibit 49. Gerber Products Company's "Objectives"

COMPANY MISSION, VALUES, AND GUIDING PRINCIPLES

MISSION — Ford Motor Company is a worldwide leader in automotive and automotive-related products and services as well as in newer industries such as aerospace, communications, and financial services. Our mission is to improve continually our products and services to meet our customers' needs, allowing us to prosper as a business and to provide a reasonable return for our stockholders, the owners of our business.

VALUES — How we accomplish our mission is as important as the mission itself. Fundamental to success for the Company are these basic values:

- **People** — Our people are the source of our strength. They provide our corporate intelligence and determine our reputation and vitality. Involvement and teamwork are our core human values.
- **Products** — Our products are the end result of our efforts, and they should be the best in serving customers worldwide. As our products are viewed, so are we viewed.
- **Profits** — Profits are the ultimate measure of how efficiently we provide customers with the best products for their needs. Profits are required to survive and grow.

GUIDING PRINCIPLES

- **Quality comes first** — To achieve customer satisfaction, the quality of our products and services must be our number one priority.
- **Customers are the focus of everything we do** — Our work must be done with our customers in mind, providing better products and services than our competition.
- **Continuous improvement is essential to our success** — We must strive for excellence in everything we do: in our products, in their safety and value — and in our services, our human relations, our competitiveness, and our profitability.
- **Employee involvement is our way of life** — We are a team. We must treat each other with trust and respect.
- **Dealers and suppliers are our partners** — The Company must maintain mutually beneficial relationships with dealers, suppliers, and our other business associates.
- **Integrity is never compromised** — The conduct of our Company worldwide must be pursued in a manner that is socially responsible and commands respect for its integrity and for its positive contributions to society. Our doors are open to men and women alike without discrimination and without regard to ethnic origin or personal beliefs.

Exhibit 50. Ford Motor Company's "Company Mission, Values, and Guiding Principles"

Goodyear's Worldwide Creed

In 1915, Goodyear adopted a creed, "Protect Our Good Name," to spur our employes to manufacture products of the highest quality and to deal fairly and courteously with our customers.

Through the years this simple credo has grown to mean much more. It serves as the basis for the corporation's social responsiveness at all levels—including our responsibilities to our employes, to the environment, to the towns and states and countries in which we do business, and to our suppliers and our customers. In fact, to everyone whose lives we touch.

"Protect Our Good Name" is not a selfless creed, for the company will fare best in a world developing in an uninterrupted and healthy manner, a world where humanitarian and economic progress will eventually become a reality for the majority of the earth's population.

The key to the world's economic development lies in greater industrialization and improved agricultural techniques to provide the necessary goods and food required by growing populations. We are convinced that the free enterprise system, while not perfect, is the most feasible means to those ends.

Today's world is a troubled world, and the free enterprise system is being challenged and tested in many places and in many ways. In this climate, we feel our creed "Protect Our Good Name" is more relevant and more valuable than ever before, as both a discipline and an inspiration.

Chairman of the Board

1974–1983

Exhibit 51. Goodyear's Worldwide Creed

and quality, is a heritage we treasure and must continue to earn everyday."

From these examples it is apparent that personality traits, as expressed in corporate mission statements, help a company develop its own personality. These are the kinds of traits—trust, integrity, honor, honesty, hard work, and a good reputation—that are important both to the company, and the employees of that company.

As might be expected, there are many other traits mentioned in mission statements. While companies indicate that these are just as important as those mentioned above, space does not permit us to discuss each individually. Therefore, rather than ignore them, we will simply include several passages from missions that express these ideas.

"To respect the dignity and inherent rights of the individual human being in all dealings with people." (Armstrong's "Principles and Objectives")

"We believe that we must be sensitive to the needs and aspirations of others . . ." (Sun Company's "The Creed We Work By")

"Simplicity in policy, principle, product design, buildings, manufacturing areas, personnel policies, and management structure will lead to a very productive organization and a successful business." (Styrotech Corporation's "Our Business Principles")

"To practice stewardship in the manufacture, marketing, use and disposal of our products." ("Dow Chemical Company Objectives")

"People are likely to be happier when they have deep personal RELIGIOUS FAITH." ("Hughes Tool Company Corporate Philosophy")

"To reflect the tenets of good taste and common courtesy in all attitudes, words and deeds." (Armstrong's "Principles and Objectives")

"Everyone has more potential than they think. A self-confident person will receive more rewards than others." ("Hughes Tool Company Corporate Philosophy")

"We should be results oriented, and all employees should be given the opportunity to express individual initiative and judgement." (Hershey Foods Corporation's "Statement of Corporate Intent")

"To continue our commitment to individual freedom and equal opportunity." ("The Dow Chemical Company Objectives")

"It is imperative that we create a climate throughout our entire organization which causes these philosophies to become a way of life." (Hershey Foods Corporation's "Statement of Corporate Intent")

12

Beyond the Mission Statement

In an earlier chapter, we defined a mission statement as a document that tells who the company is, and what the company does. While this definition is quite liberal, it has served our purposes until now.

There are some documents that fit the above definition but are not really mission statements. However, because these documents say so much about the priorities of the companies, they will be discussed here. These documents, like mission statements, help to define and clarify the priorities of the companies that publish them.

The first of these is proffered by the Squibb Corporation; its title is "The Priceless Ingredient." As was mentioned in the previous chapter, this is the story of a young man who sought the counsel of a wise man on how to get the most for what he paid. The young man was told to "Look for the Priceless Ingredient. . . . 'The Priceless Ingredient of every product is the honor and integrity of its maker.' "

This document has been a part of Squibb for many years and has become one of their trademarks. Although this document is quite old, it is still very valuable to Squibb. In its mission statement, entitled "Our Commitments," Squibb reiterates its importance by stating, "The 'Priceless Ingredient' is as priceless as ever."

A second company that has an unusual document is Southern California Edison. They have a book which is entitled "Our Management Guide." This book is made available to all of the employees to clarify the priorities of the management of the company. It consists of a series of chapters of specific topics relevant to managing the corporation. The topics include "The personality of our company needs to be well known," "The way we are organized affects the way we manage," and "Productivity and cost consciousness are our keys to profitable operations."

In the City of Bagdad lived Hakeem the Wise One, and many people went to him for counsel, which he gave freely to all, asking nothing in return.

There came to him a young man who had spent much but got little, and said: "Tell me, Wise One, what shall I do to receive the most for that which I spend?"

Hakeem answered, "A thing that is bought or sold has no value unless it contains that which cannot be bought or sold. Look for the Priceless Ingredient."

"But, what is this Priceless Ingredient?" asked the young man.

Spoke then the Wise One: "My son, the Priceless Ingredient of every product is the Honor and Integrity of its maker. Consider this name before you buy."

E.R.Squibb & Sons

Manufacturing Chemists to the Medical Profession since 1858

Exhibit 52. Squibb Corporation's "The Priceless Ingredient"

It is important that a book such as this must remain current if it is to be of maximum value. To assure this, the book is updated each time a new chairman assumes the leadership role at the company. In this way, the ideas expressed will always be in harmony with the current management of the company. In commenting on this book, William R. Gould, former chairman of Southern California Edison, had this to say:

> This booklet has been prepared to assist all of us in becoming better managers. "Our Management Guide" represents something above and beyond the thinking of any one author or individual.
>
> In a sense it represents a history of the finest experience to date in our Company—it is a record of the best know-how of our predecessors in management and of experts who have studied our company.

Another company with a document a little different than a mission statement is the Dana Corporation. It is simply entitled, "Ten Key Thoughts." Each of the thoughts expressed in this document is simple, yet thought provoking. It is essentially a condensed version of an earlier document entitled "The Forty Thoughts." The idea of condensing the forty thoughts into ten key thoughts was to make it easier for people to remember. In addition, many of the forty thoughts were in fact sub-thoughts and considered to be a part of the key thoughts.

Condensing the forty thoughts to ten key thoughts does not reflect a change in the operating philosophy of Dana. It simply reflects refinements made to keep pace with the passage of time. Both the "Ten Key Thoughts" and "The Forty Thoughts" are shown in the pages that follow.

Joseph E. Seagrams and Company is yet another company that has a document somewhat different from a true mission statement. It is a booklet, which they have published, entitled, "The Story of a Point of View." The book contains a series of advertisements the company has run over the years. All of the ads have one thing in common: they express the strongly held position that Seagram places the welfare of its customers above its own profits.

The first of these ads was published in October, 1934—less than one year after the end of Prohibition. The headline read, "We who make whiskey say: 'Drink Moderately.' " It was quite unusual for a manufacturer of distilled spirits to take such a stand on the use of their products. The public's reaction to this ad was overwhelmingly favorable. Through the years Seagram has run a wide variety of advertisements, each intended to promote the idea that the products it manufactures are to be used in a responsible manner. Seagram has made it clear that it has "an honest belief that the best interests of both the company and the consumer are best served by the moderate consumption of distilled spirits."

Forty Thoughts

Remember our purpose—to earn money for our shareholders and increase the value of their investment

Recognize people as our most important asset.	Provide autonomy.	Promote identity with Dana.	Insist on high ethical standards.
Help people grow.	Encourage entrepreneurship.	Make all Dana people shareholders.	Focus on markets.
Promote from within.	Use corporate committees, task forces.	Simplify.	Utilize assets fully.
Remember—people respond to recognition	Push responsibility down.	Use little paper.	Contain investment—buy, don't make.
Share the rewards.	Involve everyone.	Keep no files.	Balance plants, products, markets.
Provide stability of income and employment.	Make every person a manager.	Communicate fully.	Keep facilities under 500 people.
Decentralize.	Control only what's important.	Let Dana people know first.	Stabilize production.
		Let people set goals and judge their performance.	Develop proprietary products.
		Let people decide where possible.	Anticipate market needs.
		Discourage conformity.	Control cash.
		Be professional.	Deliver reliably.
		Break organizational barriers.	Do what's best for all of Dana.
		Develop pride.	

Exhibit 53. Dana Corporation's "The Forty Thoughts"

Ten Key Thoughts

- Dana people serve the shareholder.
- Dana people are our most important asset.
- Dana people accept only total quality.
- Dana people discourage centralization.
- Dana people do what's best for all of Dana.
- Dana people participate and innovate.
- Dana people compete globally.
- Dana people focus on the customer.
- Dana people communicate fully.
- Dana people are good citizens.

Exhibit 54. Dana Corporation's "Ten Key Thoughts"

For more than half a century now, the Seagram Company has taken a variety of controversial stands regarding the use of alcohol. Most of these ideas were expressed by the company before it was fashionable to do so. In 1938, Seagram began promoting the idea that responsible use of alcohol is best taught by example. In that year it ran an ad entitled, "You're a hero to your son." This was the first of the ads which carry Seagram's traditional Father's Day message.

Two topics that receive a lot of press today are drinking and driving and alcoholism. These ideas are not new to Seagram, which has been confronting these controversial topics head-on for fifty years. As early as 1935 they advertised that "Drinking and driving do not mix." In 1938 they confronted alcoholism with their advertisement entitled, "Some men should not drink."

At first glance, it would be easy to criticize any manufacturer of alcoholic beverages for promoting the use of its products, while at the same time counseling moderation. But because of the tone of these ads, Seagram has been consistently successful and has generated a great deal of consumer confidence in its products and in its company. Exhibit 55 is one of Seagram's advertisements which first appeared in *Reader's Digest* in 1973. This "handwriting" ad drew greater consumer response than any other uncouponed ad in the history of the magazine.

Another company which has a document is a little different than most mission statements is the Hughes Tool Company. In its "Corporate Philosophy," Hughes explains several ideas regarding various topics—most of which are aimed at helping its employees make the most of themselves. Before commenting on this document, let's look at some specific passages from Hughes' "Corporate Philosophy":

> "Everyone has more potential than they think. A self-confident person will receive more rewards than others. People must know themselves to be really successful. They must have courage to SELL THEIR STRENGTHS or they will accept and be handicapped by their weaknesses. Utilization of STRENGTHS will usually correct weaknesses."

> "The Hughes Tool Company believes that all human beings have a basic dignity, and we will build on their talents and strengths. It is a thrilling experience to develop PEOPLE, PRODUCTS, and PROSPERITY."

> "Looking out for one's own interest is natural and normal, but personal interest can be fully realized only through and by development of others. Happiness comes from giving knowledge, words of encouragement, guidance, constructive criticism, words of faith and material things."

Note that the purpose expressed in these ideas is to help develop people. The ideas are intended to help people develop not into better employees, but into better people. Perhaps this is because both the company and its employees benefit when people realize their full potential.

The documents mentioned in this chapter are included because they help show insight into the thoughts of the management of these companies. In some cases, these documents complement the mission statement, in other cases, they are in addition to it. And finally, for others, they simply express a point of view.

Squibb's "The Priceless Ingredient" is an extension of its mission statement "Our Commitments." "The Priceless Ingredient" has been a part of Squibb for years; its mission statement is much more recent. It could be argued, however, that Squibb's "Commitments" are an outgrowth of "The Priceless Ingredient." Although "Our Commitments" is much more specific, in many ways, the two documents say the same thing.

The party begins.

I can drive when I drink.

2 drinks later.

I can drive when I drink

After 4 drinks.

I can drive when I drunk.

After 5 drinks.

I can drin when I drin

7 drinks in all.

I can drunken drunk

The more you drink, the more coordination you lose. That's a fact, plain and simple.

Still, people drink too much and then go out and expect to handle a car.

When you drink too much you can't handle a car. You can't even handle a pen.

The House of Seagram

Exhibit 55. Joseph E. Seagram & Sons, Advertisement

The ideas expressed in Dana's "Ten Key Thoughts" and in Hughes Tool Company's "Corporate Philosophy" are auxiliary to their mission statements. Both companies have other documents more accurately labeled mission statements. The ideas expressed in these documents are no less important than those contained in their true missions, yet they are quite different. The documents included here from Southern California Edison and Joseph E. Seagram & Sons, Inc., simply express some corporate points of view.

13

The Mission within a Mission Statement

Most of the mission statements examined so far have been global mission statements. That is to say, they apply to the entire corporation, not just a part of it. They include all divisions, locations, and departments within the corporation. There are many companies however, that do not have global mission statements. They have deliberately avoided writing such a document for a variety of reasons.

For a mission statement to be accepted by the entire corporation, it must be applicable to all parts of the corporation. In today's business environment, some companies believe that such a mission statement would be too general or too vague to be of any real value. There are many situations that are not conducive to having a global mission. There are many reasons why a company might feel that a global mission statement is inappropriate for its business environment. Two examples follow.

Many of the mission statements shown in this book speak positively of the free enterprise system. While this is fine for companies located entirely in capitalist societies, it is much less desirable when one or more divisions of that company are located in a socialist country. Although a company may be located in a country with a different economic system, it is not exempt from that country's laws. It must live within the laws despite its own corporate beliefs. If a company cannot agree with the laws of the country in which it is located, it has two options: it can either work within the law to have the law changed, or it can leave.

In a similar vein, a diversified company, with divisions in totally unrelated fields, might also avoid writing a global mission statement. For a corporation with divisions involved in everything from oil exploration to movie production, a single mission statement may not be able to address all of the company's needs.

For some companies that find themselves in situations like those described above, a global mission statement might not be written. Rather, these corporations might leave it up to the local management to define their own mission. This allows the management at the local level to be more flexible in responding to their own particular needs. Whether or not a company has a global mission statement, it may still have other mission statements. Smaller groups (divisions or departments) may write their own missions defining their own individual purposes.

There are many companies that have any number of mission statements. These individual mission statements refer to parts of the total company. Each represents a division or even a single department within the company. In either case, the mission statement does not refer to the total company's business, but merely defines the role of the individual group. It explains how that group performs its task to help the company achieve its overall objectives. It is not unusual for there to be a separate mission statement for each of the individual departments within a large corporation. This mission will be specific to the individual group, defining its role within the overall corporate environment.

The individual mission statement, like the global mission statement, defines the roles of one particular group. For a group to do its job properly, it is important to recognize exactly what is expected from that group. There are many questions which must be answered—who are we? Why are we here? What should we be doing? These are the kinds of questions that can be answered in the department's mission statement.

The mission statement of a department, like the mission statement of a company, has a variety of functions. It can define the group's function, give the scope of the department's responsibilities, or define the roles and expectations for that department. In a sense, the mission statement for a department is a piece of the company's total mission statement. A company is made up of diverse groups, each with its own function. When all of these groups are performing their function, the company is operating as intended.

This is also true of the mission. When each department is accomplishing its goals as outlined in its departmental mission statement, the whole company achieves the goals as set forth in the company's global mission statement. The mission statement of an individual department has many differences from a global mission statement. A few of these differences are explained below.

First of all, the mission statement of a department tends to be more technical than a corporation's global mission statement. The details of carrying out daily activities are handled at the departmental level. These details can be quite technical in nature. The mission statement of a department reflects this increased technical nature.

Second, a departmental mission statement will tend to be more exact or specific. This may be because the roles of the people within the department are often more clearly defined. It can be more specific in defining exactly what its role is in accomplishing the company's overall mission.

A third difference between the mission statement of an individual department and that of the company is in its appearance. The mission statement for an individual department is generally not intended for distribution outside of the company. It is generally an internal document intended to properly define roles. It is less likely that such documents will be as artistically presented as their more general counterparts.

Finally, the mission statements of individual departments tend to be aimed at being more functional than global mission statements. They are more specific in defining responsibilities and explaining how the department interacts with other diverse groups. There is less of a tendency to stress the intangibles often characterized as "motherhood" and "apple pie."

Despite the differences between departmental and global mission statements, the two must agree to a certain extent. As the individual departments work together to help the company achieve its overall objective, so the mission statements of these individual departments must work within the guidelines of the company's main mission statement.

To get a better feel of what a department mission statement looks like, let's examine four.

The organizational structure for these departments is shown below:

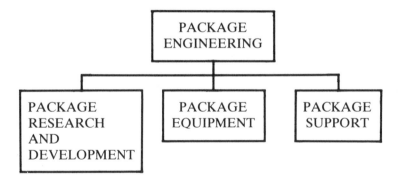

As can be seen, the packaging function is handled by four distinct groups. Briefly stated, the following summarizes the role of each of these departments.

1. *Package Engineering* is the management group that manages the other three groups.
2. *Package Research and Development* handles the component qualification for new and existing packages.
3. *Package Equipment Services* is responsible for determining and justifying the purchase of the packaging-related equipment.
4. *Package Support* serves as a support group that performs package testing and writes packaging specifications.

With four distinct groups handling the packaging activities, there could be a possibility for confusion or overlap of responsibilities. One of the tools used to avoid such situations is the departmental mission statement. Each group has its own mission very specifically defining and limiting the boundaries of each of the group's activities.

By examining each mission, several observations can be made. First of all, the mission statements of the individual departments can be combined to form a larger mission. Second, the missions serve to clarify the roles of each of these groups. Finally, the mission statements explain how the groups interact and support each other. Each of these points will be covered in more detail below.

The first point, that the combined missions form a larger mission, can best be seen by examining the individual mission statements and reviewing the organizational structure. The Package Engineering department is responsible for managing the other three packaging groups. This is reflected in both the organizational chart and the mission statement. In a sense, the mission of the Package Engineering department is the sum of the other mission statements. Although it does not get into as much detail as the others, it contains many of the same job functions. This group must rely on the other groups in the department to achieve its own mission. Only when each of these groups is successful in accomplishing its mission will the managing department achieve its mission.

Second, the department mission statements serve to clarify the roles of each of the groups. With four groups all involved in packaging activities, there is always a possibility of duplication of effort. This is avoided, however, through the use of the mission statement. The missions are quite specific: they define the individual role of each of the individual departments. When a situation occurs where there is an overlap of responsibility, the mission statement is reviewed to determine the best fit for the activity in question.

Finally, the mission statements explain how these groups interact and support each other. Each of these groups is involved with the various aspects of packaging. Each depends on the other for certain support in doing its jobs.

If a new product is introduced requiring a new technology, all groups may be involved in the qualification. The Packaging Research and Development group would qualify the new materials. The Packaging Equipment Services group would be responsible for the purchase, installation, and qualification of the new equipment. And the Package Support group would develop the specifications and perform the necessary testing to prove the process. Finally, the Package Engineering group would manage the activities of all of the groups involved to assure that all of the activities take place. The mission statement of each of these groups reflects the expectations of each of the other groups.

The preceding is a brief explanation of how four groups work together within a small group of a very successful company. By looking at the other groups in this company and examining their individual mission statement, we can see the road map that allows the company to achieve its own mission.

Package Engineering Mission Statement

Packaging Engineering is primarily responsible for providing technical packaging expertise and leadership in the design and development of new packages, changes to existing packages and the selection of packaging equipment. All items shall be evaluated for compliance to Current Good Manufacturing Practices, cost efficiency, feasibility, distribution requirements and compatibility. Packaging Engineering is also concerned with system/procedure development, maintenance and improvement/enhancement. Packaging Engineering is also responsible for the following:

- Direct and approve design, evaluation and specification of package materials assuring product and package integrity at the lowest practical cost consistent with quality, marketing, production, regulatory, and research and development requirements.

- Investigate, analyze and recommend new or improved package systems, utilizing new package concept and/or materials with the objective of both package improvement and cost reduction.

- Provide technical support in isolating package/equipment problems and the implementation of corrective action. This is a day-to-day trouble shooting function. This applies to all manufacturing plants.

- Initiate and expedite new and/or revise Packaging Bill of Materials (PBM's) and Packaging Component Specifications (PCS's).

- Determine, write and obtain approval of all packaging rework procedures.

- Provide technical support to external suppliers who require assistance.

- Provide technical support to evaluate and implement concepts developed by continuous improvement program.

Exhibit 56. "Package Engineering Mission Statement"

Packaging Engineering—Packaging Equipment Services Mission Statement

The primary mission of the Packaging Equipment Services group of Packaging Engineering department is:

"To increase productivity and sales by increasing capacity and reducing overall costs."

To meet this objective, Packaging Equipment Services's responsibilities include the following:

- To support the Packaging department with strong leadership/technical skills in the procurement of packaging equipment required to produce high quality products for all divisions.

- Integrate changes in technology with existing equipment and processes.

- Qualification/validation of all packaging equipment.

- Responsible for Capital Equipment Procurement by estimating, proposing, prepare Project Request for ACE (Appropriation for Capital Expenditure) preparation, purchases, planning fabrication, and installation of new packaging machinery, machine parts, or modification of existing packaging lines for new products.

- Monitor packaging lines capacity in order to determine when to recommend when new equipment should be ordered.

- Oversee process of acceptance, installation and start-up in compliance with performance criteria of all new packaging equipment.

- Prepare layout of lines for optimum production.

- Recommend cost reduction ideas and simplification methods/systems to improve packaging operations.

- Make recommendations concerning the need for equipment repair and the severity of such needs. Conduct cost analysis in equipment repair versus purchase of replacement equipment.

- Responsible for coordinating package equipment alterations for new products and packages.

- Establish Package Equipment Transfer approval process which results in ownership of equipment being transferred from Packaging Engineering to Packaging department.
- Active participation in Team Packaging program.

Exhibit 57. "Packaging Equipment Services Mission Statement"

Packaging Engineering—Package Support Group Mission Statement

The primary mission of the Packaging Specification and Laboratory group is to provide Packaging Laboratory, Packaging Bill of Materials (PBM's), Packaging Component Specifications (PCS's) support to Packaging Equipment and Packaging R&D groups within Packaging Engineering. To meet this mission, the Packaging Specification/Laboratory's responsibilities include the following:

- Provide technical support in isolating package and package equipment problems and the implementation of corrective action. This is a day-to-day trouble shooting function for all manufacturing plants.
- Provide technical leadership and support in the development of documentation required for packaging all Products.
- Provide for the coordination of the Packaging Engineering Laboratory resources.
- Provide technical leadership and support evaluation of all new and existing packaging component suppliers.
- Provide a consulting resource for packaging documentation for other Packaging Engineering groups.

Exhibit 58. "Package Support Group Mission Statement"

Packaging Engineering—Package Research and Development Mission Statement

Strategic contributor with technical support and services to the Operations, Marketing, and Research and Development Divisions for the structural design and development of safe and cost effective packaging systems.

- Provide complete structural package design and development support for new product packaging and transfer from Research and Development.
- Provide complete structural package design and development support to all Marketing divisions.
- Provide complete structural package design and development support to all manufacturing facilities to assure new or revised packaging components will run effectively and efficiently.
- Provide complete structural package design and development support to Packaging Equipment and Packaging Support groups within the Packaging Engineering department.
- Provide technical packaging leadership in the design and development support to Continuous Improvement Program, Team Packaging, Packaging Quality Improvement Program, and Operations Engineering.
- Provide technical packaging leadership in exploiting and evaluating new packaging technologies for packaging improvement and cost reduction.

Exhibit 59. "Package Research and Development Mission Statement"

14

Putting a Mission
Statement Together

Writing a mission statement is no easy task. Yet more and more companies are finding it desirable to do so. In this chapter we will look at some of the fundamentals of writing a corporate mission statement and what problems the author can expect to encounter.

Often when the mission statement is read, it will be evaluated. Unfortunately, much of this evaluation will be done with a great deal of skepticism. It is therefore very important that the words, thoughts, priorities, and so on be as accurate as possible, leaving as little as possible for misinterpretation.

The process of putting a mission statement together can be very difficult. There is no "right way" of doing it. The actual process will vary from company to company. The guidelines presented below are simply one way of accomplishing the task.

The process of writing a mission statement can be broken down into several distinct steps; these include:

1. Establish the basic parameters;
2. Collect and assemble possible ideas for inclusion;
3. Determine the limits;
4. Set the priorities of each statement;
5. Carefully express each of the ideas;
6. Add explanatory statements;
7. Establish the document's appearance;
8. Gain final approval.

Each of these steps will be discussed in the paragraphs which follow.

The first step in putting the mission statement together is to establish its basic parameters. Here many questions will be presented. There will be far more questions than there are answers. However, the answers to these questions are critical because they form the basis of the mission statement.

The most important and obvious first question is "What is the purpose of the mission statement?" Although obvious, this question is not an easy one. In order for the mission statement to be of any real value, there must be agreement on what it is to accomplish. It could be a guideline by which the company could run itself. Or it could more accurately be a simple description of the business in which the company wants to be involved. It could contain very specific measurable goals. Or it could contain nothing but "motherhood" and "apple pie" concepts.

Another question which must be answered up front is "Who is the audience?" Answering this question will help determine how much information can be in the mission statement. The audience may include only current employees, and therefore the information contained can be more specific. Or, if the document is to be available to outside sources, it may contain information that is less technical in nature.

A related question involves the amount of information to be contained in the mission statement. Each company has its own trade secrets that help make the company unique. This information could be dangerous if it were made available to sources outside of the company. If the mission statement reveals too much information, then certain competitive advantages will be lost. This is precisely why some companies consider their mission statements to be inside documents and do not allow them to be reprinted outside the company.

There are other valid reasons to limit the information contained in a mission statement. A company that is actively looking to expand its business into new areas would not want to limit itself in its mission statement. If the areas of business are likely to expand, it would be unwise for a company to limit its growth by being too specific in its mission statement. On the other hand, some companies have many opportunities to pursue and only limited resources. Such a company may want to limit its business to a specific area.

Another question to be answered is "How specific should the mission statement be?" While some companies are very specific in their missions, others are more vague. By reviewing the mission statements in this book we will see that companies have very different answers to this question. Some companies invite comparison with a specific, measurable guideline: "Our financial objectives also include a minimum 20% return of the year shareholders' equity and an 'A' rated balance sheet." (Ecolab's "Quest for Excellence"). Other companies set their goals against a guideline which is not so specific: "Honeywell expects profits which equal or exceed those

THE CREED WE WORK BY

A STATEMENT OF PRINCIPLES

Recognizing that business is among the institutions affecting the well-being of mankind, and that the philosophy as well as the performance of particular corporations is of proper public interest, we the Directors of Sun Company, Inc., set forth these beliefs:

 e believe human development to be the worthiest of the goals of civilization and independence to be the superior condition for nurturing growth in the capabilities of people. ▪

We believe freedom of choice is the critical requisite of any form of social organization that effectively provides for self-determination. Competition both encourages and makes practical the exercise of that freedom. And competition is in turn encouraged when meritorious achievement is recognized by commensurate reward. ▪

We believe economic competition spurred by the profit motive gives unparalleled thrust to production, provides the material base for superior living standards, and preserves the widest latitude for the exercise of individual preferences. ▪

We believe that while business cannot survive if incapable of performing profitably, its sole obligation does not consist literally of producing profits. Instead, it must also nourish values cherished by the society of which it is a part. ▪

We believe we are obligated to be responsible in conducting the affairs of Sun Company to the interests of its customers, employees and stockholders. Also, we must be responsive to the broader concerns of the public, including especially the general desire for improvement in the quality of life, equal opportunity for all, and the constructive use of natural resources. ▪

We believe we must be sensitive to the needs and aspirations of others, and that it is important we seek understanding in turn of the goals of Sun Company, its policies and the manner in which it attempts to discharge its responsibilities. Consequently, we will strive to maintain open communications with all affected by or concerned with our Company. ▪

We believe that managers of organizations hold a trust, and that their stewardship demands scrupulous treatment of the loyalties and resources committed to their direction. We acknowledge this principle as it applies specifically to us. ▪

Finally, we know that the conduct and character of our Company will depend ultimately upon the many thousands of persons who contribute to its functions. Each plays a part; each possesses a unique degree of skill and dedication; each holds and is entitled to a personal creed. It will be our conscious purpose to encourage, by precept and especially by example, competency and a common practice of fairness, honesty and integrity as the hallmark of Sun Company. ▪

SUN COMPANY

Exhibit 60. Sun Company's "The Creed We Work By"

WORTHINGTON INDUSTRIES' PHILOSOPHY

EARNINGS

The first corporate goal for Worthington Industries is to earn money for its shareholders and increase the value of their investment.

We believe that the best measurement of the accomplishment of our goal is consistent growth in earnings per share.

OUR GOLDEN RULE

We treat our customers, employees, investors and suppliers as we would like to be treated.

PEOPLE

We are dedicated to the belief that people are our most important asset.

We believe people respond to recognition, opportunity to grow and fair compensation.

We believe that compensation should be directly related to job performance and therefore use incentives, profit sharing or otherwise, in every possible situation.

From employees we expect an honest day's work for an honest day's pay.

We believe in the philosophy of continued employment for all Worthington people.

In filling job openings every effort is expended to find candidates within Worthington, its divisions or subsidiaries.

When employees are requested to relocate from one operation to another, it is accomplished without financial loss to the individual.

CUSTOMERS

Without the customer and his need for our products and services we have nothing.

We will exert every effort to see that the customer's quality and service requirements are met.

Once a commitment is made to a customer, every effort is made to fulfill that obligation.

SUPPLIERS

We cannot operate profitably without those who supply the quality raw materials we need for our products.

From a pricing standpoint we ask only that suppliers be competitive in the marketplace and treat us as they do their other customers.

We are loyal to suppliers who meet our quality and service requirements through all market situations.

ORGANIZATION

We believe in a divisionalized organizational structure with responsibility for performance resting with the head of each operation.

All managers are given the operating latitude and authority to accomplish their responsibilities within our corporate goals and objectives.

In keeping with this philosophy, we do not create corporate procedures. If procedures are necessary within a particular company operation, that manager creates them.

We believe in a small corporate staff and support group to service the needs of our shareholders and operating units as requested.

COMMUNICATION

We communicate through every possible channel with our customers, employees, shareholders and the financial community.

CITIZENSHIP

Worthington Industries practices good·citizenship at all levels. We conduct our business in a professional and ethical manner when dealing with customers, neighbors and the general public worldwide.

We encourage all our people to actively participate in community affairs.

We support worthwhile community causes.

Exhibit 61. "Worthington Industries' Philosophy"

We firmly believe that the most significant factor contributing to our Company's progress has been the strict adherence to sound principles—principles laid down by the founder and carried forward and given new dimensions by succeeding managements. Armstrong has enjoyed an unusual degree of continuity and overlapping of experience in its leadership. This, coupled with close working relationships at all levels of management, has helped to make these principles more meaningful and to assure their application.

Of almost as much importance as our principles are our basic objectives. These objectives have changed through the years only in regard to the markets served.

PRINCIPLES

1. To respect the dignity and inherent rights of the individual human being in all dealings with people.

2. To maintain high moral and ethical standards and to reflect honesty, integrity, reliability and forthrightness in all relationships.

3. To reflect the tenets of good taste and common courtesy in all attitudes, words and deeds.

4. To serve fairly and in proper balance the interests of all groups associated with the business—customers, stockholders, employees, suppliers, community neighbors, government and the general public.

OBJECTIVES

1. To manufacture and distribute in the United States and abroad a line of building products and interior furnishings—including floor coverings (resilient flooring and carpets), ceiling systems, and furniture—a variety of industrial specialties, and related services, all of which can be marketed profitably because they satisfy customer and consumer needs.

2. To earn favorable customer and consumer acceptance of these products and services by maintaining high standards of quality and dependability, by selling them at fair prices consistent with their value, and by aggressive marketing efforts.

3. To achieve consistent and profitable sales growth by

increasing manufacturing and marketing efficiency, by research pointed to the discovery of customer needs and the development of products and services to satisfy them, and by the acquisition of other enterprises that meet the objectives of the Company.

4. To earn sufficient profit on the capital employed in the enterprise to provide for continuing growth and for the payment of regular and adequate dividends to stockholders as compensation for their investment.

5. To maintain a highly productive, energetic, and loyal organization of men and women by selecting and training capable employees and by providing good working conditions, competent leadership, compensation on the basis of performance, opportunity for growth and development, and a high degree of employment security.

6. To be ethical in all dealings with suppliers and potential suppliers and, in the placement of orders, to select those sources that provide the best value to the Company, taking into account price, quality, reliability, and service.

7. To recognize a basic responsibility to the general public—community, state and nation—and to meet that responsibility by operating a business that contributes to the economic growth and strength of the economy; by providing tax support for necessary government service; by aiding worthy health, educational, and welfare institutions; by taking an active part in community affairs; and by participating in the formulation of sound public policy directed to the achievement of a social and economic climate favorable to business growth, prosperity, high employment, and national well-being.

Exhibit 62. Armstrong's Principles and Objectives

of leading international companies" (Honeywell Principles). Still other companies state goals that are more general: "To serve as good custodians of our stockholders' invested capital by enhancing its value through consistent growth in profits and return on investment" (General Signal's credo).

These are just a sampling of the questions that can be asked when a mission statement is being formed. This, however, is just the beginning. Many more questions are sure to arise—each as important as the other.

After dealing with these preliminary questions, it is time to move on to the second step in forming the mission statement: collecting and assembling possible ideas for inclusion. This is the brainstorming step where a company will try to address everything which may or may not find its way into the final mission statement. At this point all potential ideas and statements are written down. The wording is not vital at this point, nor are the length or number of potential ideas. What is important is that as many important ideas as possible be presented. In the steps that follow, these ideas will be cleaned up and the proper wording set.

Depending on the intent of the mission statement, as defined in the first step, the brainstorming step may be very long and involved, or it might be somewhat shorter in scope. And although this step is intended to collect all possible ideas, such will probably not always be the case. This step will likely be revisited several times during the writing process as new people try to get their own ideas included in the final document.

After brainstorming, the logical third step is to determine the limits of the mission statement. There will be ideas presented that are too vague or general to be included. There may be others that are too specific, giving out too much information. This is the step in which limits are drawn. The

---

Dana Policies

EARNINGS

The purpose of the Dana Corporation is to earn money for its shareholders and to increase the value of their investment. We believe the best way to do this is to earn an acceptable return by properly utilizing our assets and controlling our cash.

GROWTH

We believe in steady growth to protect our assets against inflation.

We will grow in our selected markets by implementing our market strategies.

PEOPLE

We are dedicated to the belief that our people are our most important asset. Wherever possible, we encourage all Dana people within the entire world organization to become shareholders, or by some other means, own a part of their company.

We believe people respond to recognition, freedom to participate, and the opportunity to develop.

We believe that people should be involved in setting their own goals and judging their own performance. The people who know best how the job should be done are the ones doing it.

We believe Dana people should accept only total quality in all tasks they perform.

We endorse productivity plans which allow people to share in the rewards of productivity gains.

We believe that all Dana people should identify with the company. This identity should carry on after they have left active employment.

We believe facilities with people who have demonstrated a commitment to Dana will be competitive and thus warrant our support.

We believe that wages and benefits are the concern and responsibility of managers. The Management Resource Program is a worldwide matter—it is a tool that should be used in the development of qualified Dana people. We encourage income protection, health programs, and education.

We believe that on-the-job training is an effective method of learning. A Dana manager must prove proficiency in at least one line of our company's work—marketing, engineering, manufacturing, financial services, etc. Additionally, these people must prove their ability as supervisors and be able to get work done through other people. We recognize the importance of gaining experience both internationally and domestically.

We believe our people should move across product, discipline, and organizational lines. These moves should not conflict with operating efficiency.

We believe in promoting from within. Dana people interested in other positions are encouraged to discuss job opportunities with their supervisor.

Managers are responsible for the selection, education and training of all people.

All Dana people should have their job performance reviewed at least once a year by their supervisors.

We believe in providing programs to support the Dana Style. We encourage professional and personal development of all Dana people.

PLANNING

We believe in planning at all levels.

The Policy Committee is responsible for developing the corporate strategic plan.

Each operating unit within its regional organization is responsible for a detailed five-year business plan. These business plans must support the corporate strategic plan and market strategies. These plans are reviewed annually.

Commitment is a key element of the Dana Management Style. This commitment and performance will be reviewed on a monthly basis by the appropriate regional operating committee and on a semi-annual basis during Mid-Year Reviews.

ORGANIZATION

We discourage conformity, uniformity and centralization.

We believe in a minimum number of management levels. Responsibility should be pushed as far into the organization as possible.

Organizational structure must not conflict with doing what is best for all of Dana.

We believe in an organizational structure that allows the individual maximum freedom to perform and participate. This will stimulate initiative, innovation, and the entrepreneurial spirit that is the cornerstone of our success.

We believe in small, highly effective, support groups to service specialized needs of the Policy Committee and the world organization at large as requested. We believe in task forces rather than permanent staff functions.

We do not believe in company-wide procedures. If an organization requires procedures, it is the responsibility of the manager to create them.

CUSTOMERS

Dana is a global company focused on markets and customers. We compete globally by supplying products and services to meet the needs of our customers in our selected markets.

We are dedicated to the belief that we have a responsibility to be leaders in our selected markets.

We believe it is absolutely necessary to anticipate our customers needs for products and services of the highest quality. Once a commitment is made to a customer, every effort must be made to fulfill that obligation.

It is highly desirable to outsource a portion of our production needs. Outsourcing increases our competitiveness and protects the stability of employment for our people. It also protects our assets and assures performance to our customers.

Dana People throughout the organization are expected to know our customers and their needs.

COMMUNICATION

We will communicate regularly with shareholders, customers, Dana people, general public, and financial communities.

It is the job of all managers to keep Dana people informed. Each manager must decide on the best method of communication. We believe direct communication with all of our people eliminates the need for a third party involvement. All managers shall periodically inform their people about the performance and plans of their operation.

CITIZENSHIP

The Dana Corporation will be a good citizen worldwide. All Dana people are expected to do business in a professional and ethical manner with integrity.

Laws and regulations have become increasingly complex. The laws of propriety always govern. The General Counsel and each General Manager can give guidance when in doubt about appropriate conduct. It is expected that no one would willfully violate the law and subject themselves to disciplinary action.

We encourage active participation of all of our people in community action.

We will support worthwhile community causes consistent with their importance to the good of Dana people in the community.

The Policy Committee
Dana Corporation

Approved by The Board of Directors
Dana Corporation

Exhibit 63. Dana Corporation's "Policies"

ideas should be pared down so that the mission statement does not become a book. Many ideas will be omitted. Others will be combined with similar ideas. It is in this step that the actual mission statement begins to take form. Here it starts to take shape as something that truly represents the company.

A fourth step involves establishing a priority among the assembled ideas. This may either be a formal priority statement or it may be informal, but it is important that some order be given to the ideas. When a formal priority is given, each of the statements may begin with a phrase defining the priority such as, "Our first responsibility is . . ." Even when there is no formal prioritization, there will be an implied one. It is natural to believe that the first idea presented is the most important, and that ideas that follow are less important. Although not always true, this will be the perception of many who read the document.

The fifth step is to carefully express each of the statements to be included in the document. It is important that the thoughts be worded as clearly as possible. Remember that there will be a tendency to view the mission statement with a skeptical eye. It is therefore very important that there be no areas left open for misinterpretation, and that nothing negative be implied in what is said.

An additional benefit to careful wording of each of the ideas is that it allows individual ideas to be combined into a more global idea. Two or more closely related ideas can be joined to form a single thought.

The sixth step in putting the mission statement together involves adding explanations for certain ideas presented. These may include explaining what the document is supposed to do and what it is not. Or it could explain a certain point in more detail, such as defining why profits are important. Or it could explain that all of the ideas presented are equally important and indivisible.

The seventh step in putting together the mission statement is to establish the look of the document. This will vary depending on many factors including the audience and the purpose of the document. The looks will be quite different for a departmental mission statement and a document intended to be displayed on the wall of corporate headquarters.

The mission statement is a reflection of the company. For this reason it is often as difficult to establish the look as it is to write the document. The company that proudly displays its mission statement wants to put its best foot forward. The overall look of the document is important in doing so. Details such as the typestyle, the location and size of the company's logo, and even the amount of white space are important in determining the overall look.

The final step of putting a mission statement together involves getting final approval for the document. Although this step is listed last, it is more likely to come up many times during the entire process. There may have

TEXACO'S GUIDING PRINCIPLES AND OBJECTIVES

The principles and objectives which guide Texaco in doing the best possible job of finding and producing increasing quantities of oil and natural gas, refining superior products, transporting and marketing products efficiently and economically, and further improving its operations and products through continuing research, are:

TO DELIVER to customers only products of proven high quality at fair prices and to serve them in such a manner as to earn their continuing respect, confidence, and loyalty, both before and after sale.

TO BE financially sound and responsible, pay a fair return to shareholders for the use of their capital, maintain a record of productivity and profits which will enable the Company to attract new capital and continue to grow and expand its earning power, and through inspired leadership and effective teamwork strive to be the most highly respected company in industry.

TO MAINTAIN a high level of employe morale through fostering by example an atmosphere of hard work, recognize dignity of the individual by treating every person in the Company with respect and courtesy, provide opportunities for employes to develop and advance to the utmost of their capabilities, encourage and carefully consider all suggestions from employes and if not acceptable explain reasons why to employe, pay compensation which compares favorably with others in the industry, and provide safe and efficient places in which to work.

TO OBEY all laws, be a good corporate citizen and willingly assume our share of the responsibilities in communities where we operate both at home and abroad, conduct our affairs in a capable and friendly manner so that everyone who comes in contact with us will find it pleasant to do business with us, observe the highest moral and ethical standards in carrying on our business, and keep our organization a fine example of the American system of freedom and opportunity.

TO MAINTAIN free and open channels for the mutual exchange of information between management, stockholders, employes, retailers, customers, and others having a proper interest in the affairs of the Company, work constructively toward securing public understanding and acceptance of the Company's policies and performance, defend the Company against unwarranted and unjustified criticism and attack, support industry efforts to resolve mutual problems in the area of public affairs, cooperate in other activities undertaken for the benefit of the industry as a whole where these activities do not involve competitive or operating matters or infringe upon the Company's right to independent action.

Exhibit 64. "Texaco's Guiding Principles and Objectives"

Tektronix Statement of Corporate Intent

To Provide Unmatched Value in the Product and Service We Offer Customers.

Customer satisfaction is what keeps us in business. "Value" is the key word here — a concept that includes not only product usefulness and quality, but also cost.

Some superlatives aren't always worth achieving; for instance, "The finest in craftsmanship" matters little to the person who can't afford and doesn't need it. The one superlative we do endorse is "unmatched value" — for that insures a satisfied customer.

We must be customer-oriented at all levels and in all jobs. In product development, for instance, we must be aware of customer needs very early, so the necessary products are available soon enough to keep new technology alive and growing. Historically, Tektronix customers have come to expect that.

Every Tektronix employee should know that his or her job relates to customer satisfaction.

To Recognize the One Limitless Resource: the Individual and Collective Potential of the Human Being.

To Provide Employees with Maximum Opportunity to Exceed Their Own Expectations.

"The right person in the right job" means we have to keep at two seemingly opposed tasks: One is to grow people, helping the individual expand to meet the next day's challenges — and, through effective grouping, attain larger and longer-term goals. The other is to increase the challenges themselves, so the job we offer will extend or even surpass existing skills. Allowing a person to remain bigger than the job invites boredom; allowing the job to remain bigger than the person invites frustration. The personal rewards and satisfactions that come from a long-term affiliation with the company are earned through a

sustained high level of performance. People want to do a good job. We seek to enable their personal contribution toward company goals that they see as coinciding with their own.

Employee contributions are of different kinds. Each is encouraged and rewarded differently. Overall company results are achieved through constant improvement in individual performance; we recognize this contribution through a merit-based system of pay and promotion. The company benefits from a team effort of interdependent cooperative activity; we recognize this through profit sharing. Stable employment and long-term affiliation also contribute to the company's success; we recognize this through certain employee benefits that increase with tenure.

To Achieve Continued Improvement in the Use of Company Resources.

The productive and innovative use of company resources is critical to long-term success. Our organization must encourage the risk-taking essential to developing new and better ways of operating. We need an organization, and employees, committed to making things happen. A combination of excitement and aggressiveness is necessary if we are to be first to move forward in new directions others have not perceived.

Our products' success must be measured in terms of innovations as well as profitability — bringing into being something of unique value. Moreover, we must have a continuous flow of such products to be competitive. Leadership in the fast-growing electronics industry demands that we anticipate the changing needs of our customers and respond to those needs with superior products.

The company, as it grows, must take advantage of its increased experience. Asset utilization needs to improve. Unit costs need to decline. We cannot be satisfied with our performance. We must seek continuous improvement.

To Grow As a Means of Maintaining and Renewing Vitality.

Growth has many aspects: sales, profits, assets, technology, job challenge, employee earnings, new products and services, personal knowledge and confidence. No one of these must be allowed to eclipse the others; a proper balance among them must always be struck.

To remain static in an expanding field is clearly to fall behind. But bigness just for bigness' sake is not a reasonable goal; nor is rapid growth by itself a reliable measure of strength. Orderly growth is far more indicative — and orderly growth will result as we effectively meet our other objectives.

To Insure that Corporate Objectives, Wherever Possible, Enhance the Goals of the Immediate and Larger Communities of Which We Are a Part.

We believe that a corporation best serves the interests of society by being successful. Such success means providing high-value products to customers, creating stimulating and stable employment opportunities, and generating a superior return to investors.

We recognize the opportunity to create a successful business occurs in a larger context. The world has become far too small, and its parts too interrelated for us to set objectives without being mindful of their effect on others. As a local, a national and a global citizen, we must continually keep abreast of the social, political and economic strivings of those about us.

Tektronix will continue not only to adhere to the spirit and letter of the law, but also to lead the way in corporate citizenship, contributing as broadly as possible to the common welfare; for instance, giving of its resources to help solve social problems, to aid and encourage

education, and to support actively the individual employee's involvement in the community.

To Achieve Superior Levels of Profitability.

Tektronix must maintain a high level of profitability in order to meet the expectations of our stakeholders: customers, employees, shareowners, suppliers, the general public. A long-term commitment to superior profitability is an essential condition for our growth and development as an organization. This requires that Tektronix utilize the wealth-producing capacities of its resources to the fullest. In an economic sense, profit results when Tektronix' resources generate a return higher than the cost of capital. Superior profitability is the source for the company's growth, for investments in new products and technologies, for the creation of meaningful jobs, and for community contributions. Profitability is an essential corporate objective, as well as the result of having carefully chosen and effectively met other objectives.

We do not expect the same profitability on all products, or from all segments of the company, at all times in a product's life, or in all economic circumstances. We do expect our various product lines to be sufficiently innovative to generate a high return for the resources invested over their life cycle.

In a public, profit-sharing company, attention understandably may tend to focus on near-term results. However, we must not overly restrain investment that is directed toward the future, particularly in research and development, in favor of short-term gain; our objective is continuing long-term profitability. Thus, a major charge placed on Tektronix' managers is to achieve the proper balance between near-term results and long-range perspectives.

Exhibit 65. "Tektronix Statement of Corporate Intent"

to be approval given at each step along the way. The approval process is often thought to be a never ending process. Even after approval is given for certain wording, for example, the wording may be reconsidered time and time again to improve the final product.

Getting a final blessing on the document will be achieved differently depending on the company. For some companies, the final approval will be done at the board level, and the resulting document distributed to the employees as the official mission statement. In other companies, the rough draft will be sent to employees soliciting comments and suggestions for improvement. In still other cases, someone in between these levels will have the authority to approve or disapprove of the document.

Each company has its own style. Each has its unique way in which it recognizes problems and opportunities. Many companies feel that it is important for the people within the organization to recognize the company's individual style. The mission can be one way of addressing or defining how the management of that company chooses to run its business.

It may not be important for each of the employees to commit the mission statement to memory; what can be far more important is for them to understand the environment that the document defines. The future of the company may well depend on how well the individuals understand and apply the company's own unique style to their everyday activities.

15

The Final Word

There has been quite a bit of material printed about mission statements and their value or lack of value. Yet one question remains: what does all of it mean? There are those who are in favor of mission statements, and there are those who could not care less. But what does all of this really mean?

To answer this question, let's review where mission statements originate. They are documents that are written internally. They are written by people who are employed by the company, hence, they can be quite biased. However, the ultimate determination of a company's character is not what it says about itself but what it does. Companies are judged by actions, not words. Each company sets its own priorities and determines for itself the criteria by which it wants to be judged.

A mission statement gives an indication of what the management of a company feels is important. It bespeaks priorities, and how the company wants the business run. The mission statement is a guideline intended to demonstrate the management's philosophy. It is intended to show what that company feels is important.

The value of a mission statement is most evident when words are transformed into actions. If the mission statement is to be of real value it must have an effect on those who champion it.

Obviously, not all people within a given company follow their mission statement with equal intensity. While some believe in them strongly, others view them with skepticism. It seems evident that the more strongly an employee believes in the mission statement, the more likely that person is to follow it. Therefore it is in the best interest of the company that believes in its mission statement to reinforce that belief among those with whom it shares a relationship.

A mission statement contains guidelines, not laws. Yet similar to laws, these guidelines vary in intensity. For example, the punishment for failure to comply with laws varies across the board. Violating the speed limit carries a penalty directly related to the extent of the violation. Exceeding the speed limit by twenty-five miles per hour usually carries a more severe penalty than exceeding it by ten miles per hour. And both penalties are less severe than that for a violent crime against another person.

Similarly, the failure to comply with the strict interpretation of a mission statement varies. The punishment for violating a code for ethics is different from not "treating others as we would be treated."

What is important in evaluating a mission statement is to consider the intent of these documents. Are they intended as public relations documents? Or are they honest beliefs of a corporation's management? Questions like these relate to the value of these documents.

Like people, many corporations have a desire to improve themselves and to improve their lot in life. They do this in different ways, an example of which is the number of New Year's resolutions made each year. While a few of these resolutions are kept, many others are not. Yet year in, and year out, the making of resolutions is quite popular. In the end, if people become better by making changes in their lives by keeping resolutions, who is to criticize them for doing so?

A mission statement has many of the same qualities of the New Year's resolution. A mission statement puts forth guidelines intended to help a company to become a better company. Similarly, New Year's resolutions are intended to help people become better people. Whether or not a given company actually follows its mission statement 100 percent of the time is not the point. The point is that many companies are trying to improve themselves and maximize their contributions to society. Mission statements have been around for a long time. As stated earlier, there are examples of mission statements as far back as biblical times. They will probably continue to exist as people and companies attempt to achieve perfection.

In evaluating mission statements of companies, let's review those things which companies are trying to encourage. They are trying to achieve the basic things considered positive in our society. They are aiming at improving such things as:

1. *Employees*—Corporations are made up of people, and these people are often considered the most important asset. Both the corporation and its employees have responsibilities to each other.

2. *Profits*—Profits are a key to our economic system that make the system work. By accepting free enterprise as our economic system profits are viewed as a positive measure of a corporation's contribution.

3. *Community*—A corporation is a member of the community in which it is located. As a member of that community, many corporations feel they have certain obligations to support the community, its activities, and the environment it shares with that community.

4. *Customers*—The customer is free to choose from the products and services of many companies. By choosing to purchase from a specific company, the customer essentially votes for that company. Knowing this, companies must pay close attention to customers' needs to survive.

5. *Quality and Excellence*—Quality and excellence are goals common to many companies. Such companies believe that obtaining a high level of both quality and excellence will lead to a win-win situation for all parties involved in the business relationship.

6. *Personality Traits*—Just as people have individual personalities, so too do companies. A company made up of people will develop a personality similar to the personalities of those people. It is therefore in the best interest of the company and its people to develop personality traits considered positive in that business environment.

There is nothing earth shattering about the items listed above. They are the logical, positive details most companies recognize as important. Some are idyllic intangibles not unlike "apple pie" and "motherhood." They are also the kinds of details that can be easily forgotten. Often a fine line exists between the company that is extremely successful and the company that is just barely getting by. Often the difference can be attributed to close attention to details. A mission statement can reinforce the desire to do just that—to pay attention to details.

Each of the details presented in mission statements, although vital, must be considered as a part of a whole management philosophy. Paying attention to only one of these aspects could be as deadly as not considering any. The mission statement contains many elements that must be prioritized. It is up to the management of the corporation to determine the balance that best fits the needs of that particular corporation.

A mission statement will not make an unsuccessful company magically successful. Nor will the lack of a mission statement turn a successful company into an unsuccessful one. Again, a company is measured not by what it says, but rather, by what it does. Whether a mission is written or merely understood may not be critical. What is important is that the company follows good business practices.

There is at least one study (shown in the appendix) suggesting that companies with mission statements have performed very well over a sustained period of time. These companies have had growth in profits far outpacing those companies making up the Dow Jones industrial average over the same period. The mission statement may or may not have helped these companies achieve this success, yet a lot can be said for the idea of following the lead of successful companies.

Each company has its own reason for being in business. The reasons vary across industries and within industries. In closing let's review a few of the hopes of companies as expressed in their mission statements.

"Our role at Celestial Seasonings is to play an active part in making this world a better place. . . . " (Celestial Seasonings' Statement of Beliefs)

"To make this world a better place for our having been in business." (Dow Chemical Company Objectives)

"We expect to make this world a better place to live. We make products that extend human capability, freeing people from drudgery and helping them achieve more than they could alone." (Apple Computer Values)

Appendix:
Reflections

On November 16, 1983, about a year had passed since the TYLENOL®
tamperings. On that day, Jim Burke, Chairman of Johnson & Johnson, was
presented with an award by the Advertising Council. In accepting the award,
Mr. Burke spoke about the poisonings and the role of "Our Credo" in
helping the company deal with the crisis.

The speech gives quite a bit of insight into the thoughts and actions of a
man whose company was put to a severe test. During the crisis there was
little time to evaluate the options available. One year later, after the dust
had settled, there was ample time for evaluation.

A transcript of that speech follows. It has been reprinted here with the
permission of Mr. Burke and Johnson & Johnson.

Thank you, Frank Cary, Bob Beck, the officers, Board, and members
of the Advertising Council. There simply is no award that could mean more
to me than this one—in part, because of my intense admiration for the
work of the Ad Council.

Leverage is a favorite "buzz word" for all of us in business. As a matter
of fact a lot of what we do in managing our businesses has to do with
leverage—leveraging our assets—whether we are talking about the balance
sheet, brand names, or the brain power of our people. I know of nowhere
that leverage has been practiced with such extraordinary success than by
the Ad Council. To take less than $2 million and to leverage it into more
than $700 million dollars' worth of advertising—and all in the interest of
the public—the idea itself is truly staggering.

I salute the Ad Council for what you have done for this country over
the past 40 years!

And try to explain the Ad Council's unique public service to someone from another country. I have. It's incomprehensible to them. In truth, it could not happen anywhere in the world in the way it has here because our capitalistic system is also unique.

And that is what I would like to comment on tonight. I would like to advance the premise that public service is not a thing apart, but implicit in the charter of every American corporation. It is, in truth, its very reason for being. That's what makes our enterprise system so special.

I would like to describe to you how that philosophy became explicit at Johnson & Johnson, how it served us well for over a generation, and how it was dramatically tested by the TYLENOL® tragedies.

But I also want to emphasize that these beliefs are not singular to Johnson & Johnson but are understood by most corporations, and that they are understood exceptionally well by quite a few. I have some evidence that suggests that those companies who organize their businesses around a broad concept of public service over the long run provide superior performance for their stockholders.

But first let me offer you a quotation which crystallizes these thoughts:

> "Institutions, both public and private exist because the people want them, believe in them, or at least are willing to tolerate them. The day has passed when business was a private matter—if it ever really was. In a business society, every act of business has social consequences and may arouse public interest. Every time a business hires, builds, sells or buys, it is acting for the people as well as for itself, and it must accept full responsibility for its acts . . . "

That was written right after World War II by a young brigadier general who had just served as head of the Small War Plants Board in Washington. His name—Robert W. Johnson.

It was part of a preamble to a document he entitled simply: "Our Credo."

I have been presumptuous enough to include a copy in your program tonight. It sounds a little pompous at first glance, and there is no need to read it now, but essentially, what this document does is articulate our responsibilities to all of those in society who are dependent on us.

First, to our customers—doctors, nurses, patients, and mothers who buy our products and services.

Second, to our employees whose creative energies are responsible for those same products and services.

Next, to our communities—not just where our plants and offices are, but all the various communities we deal with, including the community of man.

And finally to our stockholders who invest their money in our enterprise.

We have often been asked why we put our stockholder last, and our answer has always been that, if we do the other jobs properly, the stockholders will always be well served. The record would suggest that this is the case.

These guiding principles were disseminated among our employees in 1947.

A generation later, in 1975, some of us became concerned as to whether, in fact, we were practicing what we preached.

We had become a large and complex corporation, with well over 100 companies around the world, each with its own separate mission.

In corporate headquarters we were concerned that the Credo perhaps had greater meaning to us than to those who were ultimately responsible for managing our various businesses around the world.

So we tried an experiment. We invited 24 of our managers from the United States and overseas here—to the Waldorf, as a matter of fact,—for a meeting to challenge the Credo.

I opened the meeting with an observation that the document was hanging in most of our offices around the world. If we were not committed to it, it was an act of pretension and ought to be ripped off the walls. I challenged the group to recommend whether we should get rid of it, re-write it, or commit to it as is.

The meeting was a turn-on, a genuine happening, as these managers struggled with the issues that the Credo defined.

What we discovered was that we had a set of guiding principles far more powerful than we had imagined.

This was the beginning of a series of Credo challenge meetings to include all of our key management from around the world. Dave Clare, our president, and I chaired these sessions over the next three years. The result— the reworded document in your programs tonight.

The basic philosophy is unchanged. Many words stayed the same; others were changed substantively; some just modernized. Some of the responsibilities were expanded to take cognizance of a much more complicated world.

In June of 1979 we brought the managers of over 150 companies from all over the world to New York. The centerpiece of that meeting was the revitalized Credo—a statement of purpose that everyone now not only understood, but had had the chance to contribute to.

On September 29 last year we learned with a terrifying suddenness that inexplicably someone had chosen one of our products—TYLENOL®—as a murder weapon.

Thus began what was to become for us "an unremitting nightmare," and one that required literally dozens of people to make hundreds of decisions in painfully short periods of time.

Even when we had time for careful consideration, most of our decisions were complicated, involving considerable risk, and we had no historical precedence to rely on.

As you know, we have received much praise for our handling of the "TYLENOL® Affair." Certainly we are proud of the heroic job done by our people at McNeil Consumer Products and all of those from their sister companies who worked so tirelessly to help them during those difficult weeks.

And I would like to take this opportunity to thank our associates at Compton Advertising, and to Young and Rubicam's, Burson Marsteller, our friends and associates in the trade, in our industry, in government and, of course, the media.

We are grateful to all of you who helped in so many specific ways, and also for the outpouring of sympathy and support we felt from everyone. It was a great source of strength during the ordeal.

However, all of us at McNeil Consumer Products and Johnson & Johnson truly believe that the guidance of the Credo played the most important role in our decision-making.

And here let me suggest you take the Credo home with you tonight and read it. Ask yourselves, with a statement like that, if we had any alternative but to do what we did during the TYLENOL® tragedy.

Ask yourselves how the TYLENOL® customer, the Johnson & Johnson employee, the public, the stockholder would have felt. What would your attitude today be toward Johnson & Johnson if we hadn't behaved the way we did?

And, of course, the important thing that the TYLENOL® affair reaffirmed is the intrinsic fairness of the American public.

A remarkable poll by the Roper organization taken 3 months after the tragedy showed 93% of the public felt Johnson & Johnson handled its responsibility either very well or fairly well. But the public also gave very high marks to the Food and Drug Administration, the law enforcement agencies, the drug industry in general, and the media! The public knew that all these institutions were working—together—and in their interest!

And what did our consumers do? They gave us back our business. A year ago tonight we had but a fraction left of one of the most valuable franchises ever built. Our latest Neilsen, taken in July–August (1983), shows TYLENOL® has regained over 90% of the business we enjoyed prior to the tragedies.

A reassuring and exhilarating outcome.

Of course, the TYLENOL® story is also unique. But it dramatically reaffirms a philosophy that is not, which is—serving the public is what any business is all about.

That philosophy has been articulated and infused into the "cultures" by the founders and builders of many of our most successful American businesses.

Montesquieu, the French philosopher-historian, wrote, and I quote: "In the infancy of society, the chiefs of state shape institutions; later the institutions shape the chiefs of state."

I have long harbored the belief that the most successful corporations in this country—the ones that have delivered outstanding results over a long period of time—were driven by a simple moral imperative—serving the public in the broadest possible sense better than their competition.

In preparation for receiving this award, I have attempted to find convincing evidence to support this contention. Since this was the thirtieth anniversary of this award, I decided to look at companies who have been in existence for at least that long and, at the same time, fulfilled two very rigid criteria:

First, they had to have a written, codified set of principles stating the philosophy that serving the public was central to their being.

And second, solid evidence that these ideas had been promulgated and practiced for at least a generation by their organizations.

My staff worked with The Business Roundtable's Task Force on Corporate Responsibility and The Ethics Resource Center in Washington, D.C. in compiling the list.

We found 26 such companies—quite a few of which, I might add, had received this Public Service Award. We then looked at the performance of these same companies in terms of profits and rewards to the stockholders over the 30–year period.

We had to drop 11 companies from the 26 for lack of comparable data— Prudential because it is a mutual company with no stockholders; Levi Strauss, Johnson's Wax and Hewlett-Packard because they were private corporations 30 years ago; McDonald's because it didn't even exist—and so on. But the 15 remaining companies still deliver an impressive record.

First—profits. These companies showed an 11% growth in profits compounded over 30 years! (The Ad Council Award winners in the group showed exactly the same growth rate.) That happens to be better than three times the growth of the Gross National Product, which grew at 3.1% during the same period.

To understand the effect of that difference in compound rate of growth over 30 years—the GNP is now 2½ times greater than it was 30 years ago. The net income of these companies is 23 times greater!

And how about the stockholder?

If anyone of you had invested $30,000 in a composite of the Dow Jones 30 years ago, it would be worth $134,000 today.

If you had invested the same $30,000—$2,000 in each of these 15 companies instead—your $30,000 would be worth over $1,000,000! $1,021,861 to be exact! (If the Dow had grown at the same rate as these companies, it would be over 9000—9399 to be exact.)

The results are, at the very least, provocative.

Michael Novak, in his book THE THEOLOGY OF THE CORPO-RATION, talks about democratic capitalism as the system that has given the United States unparalleled wealth, freedom, and cultural richness. But he also says, and I quote: "Nothing guarantees that this system will endure forever. It is an experiment. Our failure to defend it well, with spirit and with intelligence, would be an unforgivable failure—a tragedy to the world."

I began my remarks talking about leverage and would like to end on the same thought.

I think the lesson in the TYLENOL® experience, as well as the record of these 15 companies over the past 30 years is the same, and that is that we as businessmen and women have extraordinary leverage on our most important asset—Goodwill—the Goodwill of the public. If we make sure our enterprises are managed in terms of their obligations to society, that is also the best way to defend this democratic capitalistic system that means so much to all of us.

Thank you.

Index

About the Author

THOMAS A. FALSEY is Senior Project Engineer/Packaging at Marion Laboratories, Inc. and a freelance business writer.